Advance Praise for *Burnout a*

"*Burnout and Self-Care in Social Work* is an essential read for students and mental health professionals. Smullens delves into the primary factors that can lead to burnout and offers research-backed strategies for self-care. The guidebook taps an unmet need of those who work in mental health, providing a pathway to happiness and a long-lasting career."

AARON T. BECK, MD
Emeritus Professor of Psychiatry
University of Pennsylvania
Father of cognitive therapy

"This book was born out of the tragedy of a six-year-old child shackled to her bed and starved by her parents. The judge who heard the case ignored the recommendations of a newly minted social worker—the author. How many similar stories can professionals witness before empathy coarsens and compassion dulls? SaraKay Smullens has lived through all of this and has written a book for those working the frontlines. She combines a wealth of personal experience with scholarly analysis. The book is both practical and inspirational, a gift to her profession."

ROGER GOULD, MD
Psychiatrist and author

"SaraKay Smullens has seen far too many committed social workers leave the work they arduously trained for frustrated, exhausted, and burned out, and she is determined to do something about it. Through thorough research on burnout and self-care, a survey of social workers offering real-life observations, excellent case examples, reflective questions, and a sprinkling of her own experiences, she has written a book that clarifies, educates, guides, and uplifts. This book underscores the breadth, depth, commitment, and passion of a much underestimated profession."

LINDA MAY GROBMAN, MSW, ACSW, LSW
Publisher/editor, *The New Social Worker* magazine

"SaraKay Smullens's astutely written book is a gift to everyone whose demanding occupations—particularly those involving traumatized and vulnerable men, women, and children—often lead to the emotional and physical inoperability known as burnout. In her two-part examination, SaraKay deftly explores burnout and self-care through professional, personal, social, and physical interactions, illuminating the origin and toll of the three major causes of burnout—compassion fatigue, countertransference, and vicarious trauma (and how vulnerable all are to their impact). She illuminates the road to achieving and maintaining 'compassion satisfaction' through introspection, respectful boundaries, and empathy (rather than sympathy or pity) and creatively documents self-care alternatives. As a medical writer and reporter, I applaud this thoroughly researched, evidence-based journey, where obstacles are faced, understood, and removed, resulting in renewal for practitioners and new options and possibilities for their clients."

GLORIA HOCHMAN
Bestselling author, with Patty Duke, of
A Brilliant Madness: Living with Manic-Depressive Illness

"Finally! A book that nurtures, prepares, and strengthens an internal experience and offers terrific strategies and smiles for a wide audience in a familiar voice we deeply respect. We are so pleased to endorse our mom's, stepmom's, and mom-in-law's book."

ELISABETH JOY LAMOTTE, LICSW
University of Pennsylvania
KATHYANNE SCHLESS, ESQ.
University of Pennsylvania
ELIZABETH SMULLENS BRASS, MFA
Art Institute of Chicago
DEBORAH BLOCK, MFA
Temple University

"When social workers choose to help the most vulnerable children and adults, they are exposed to intense demands for compassion, understanding, and love. The ability of the professional to function in the service of others can be compromised by burnout, fatigue, and his or her own need to be valued. No better guide can be found than SaraKay Smullens's book on how the therapist, educator, and counselor can remain healthy to be helpful. It should become a basic text in this neglected field."

DAVID SACHS, MD
Emeritus Clinical Professor of Psychiatry Hahnemann University

"I have known and admired SaraKay Smullens for over four decades. Her latest work is illustrative of why she is the wisest woman I know. In these draining, complicated times, as burnout seems to wait in the wings for us, this text offers crucial information. If you are not in SaraKay's field, skim (or skip) the detailed research and read the clear explanations and case studies. Study the three primary causes of burnout, pinpoint where you may be vulnerable, and learn what to do about it. SaraKay describes the potential of the self and how to achieve what she calls "an emotional sense of direction" in illuminating ways. Her exploration of empathy is a guide to mature, compassionate relationships. As you read, your eyes may mist, but you will also smile. This book is about far more than burnout and self-care. This book is about love."

BONNIE STRAUSS
Journalist and documentary filmmaker

BURNOUT
and
SELF-CARE
in Social Work

**A GUIDEBOOK FOR STUDENTS AND THOSE IN MENTAL HEALTH
AND RELATED PROFESSIONS**

SARAKAY SMULLENS

NASW PRESS
National Association of Social Workers
Washington, DC

DARRELL P. WHEELER, PhD, MPH, ACSW, *President*
ANGELO McCLAIN, PhD, LICSW, *Chief Executive Officer*

Cheryl Y. Bradley, *Publisher*
Julie Gutin, *Managing Editor*
Sarah Lowman, *Project Manager*
Stella Donovan, *Acquisitions Editor*
Wayson Jones, *Copyeditor*
Juanita Doswell, *Proofreader*
Bernice Eisen, *Indexer*

Cover by Metadog Design Group
Interior design and composition by Electronic Quill Publishing Services
Printed and bound by Integrated Books International

First impression: July 2015
Second impression: July 2016
Third impression: October 2018
Fourth impression: October 2019

© 2015 by the NASW Press

The following article from *The New Social Worker* has been adapted with permission from
White Hat Communications and *The New Social Worker*: Smullens, S. (2012). What I wish
I had known: Burnout and self-care in our social work profession. *The New Social Worker,
19*(4), 6–9.

Photograph of the author by Sharon Wohlmuth Teacher, Philadelphia.

Library of Congress Cataloging-in-Publication Data

Smullens, SaraKay.
    Burnout and self-care in social work : a guidebook for students and those in mental
health and related professions / SaraKay Smullens.
        pages cm
    Includes bibliographical references and index.
        ISBN 978-0-87101-462-7 — ISBN 0-87101-462-9 1. Social workers—Job stress.
    2. Social service—Psychological aspects. 3. Burn out (Psychology) I. Title.
        HV40.35.S598 2015
        361.301'9—dc23
                                                                                2015019002

Printed in the United States of America

For all students of social work,
wherever you are studying,
and for those entering our and other
mental health and related professions

Note from a Client

In our first meeting my client, looking away, handed me a note.

It read, "I have no voice. It became too much. I began dying years ago. No one noticed."

I responded with a note, "Until you find your voice, do you want me to write to you? Or may I speak?"

"Will you go away?" she wrote.

We made eye contact. I moved my head, "No."

"Do you believe I can find my voice?" she wrote. And continued, "If so, say it."

"Yes."

Table of Contents

About the Author

 **SaraKay Smullens, LCSW, ACSW, BCD, CGP, CFLE,** whose private and pro bono clinical social work practice is in Philadelphia, is a certified group psychotherapist and family life educator. She is a recipient of a Lifetime Achievement Award from NASW-PA, which recognized her long-standing community organization, advocacy, and activism, as well as the codification of patterns of emotional abuse and the development of a therapeutic model to address it. SaraKay is the founder of the Philadelphia initiative The Sabbath of Domestic Peace, which identified clergy as a "missing link" in addressing domestic violence, devoting itself to clergy involvement and education that prayer alone would not save lives and that couples in distress, due to abuse and violence, could not be seen together. SaraKay has published in peer-reviewed journals, is the best-selling author of *Whoever Said Life Is Fair?: A Guide to Growing Through Life's Injustices* and *Setting YourSelf Free: Breaking the Cycle of Emotional Abuse in Family, Friendships, Work, and Love*, and blogs for *The Huffington Post*. Her professional papers and memorabilia are divided between the Archives of the University of Pennsylvania, Goucher College, and the John F. Kennedy Presidential Library. SaraKay's professional life continues to be devoted to highlighting destructive societal forces through education, advocacy, and activism.

Foreword

I love social work. Social work is my passion. It feels good to help people. I absolutely adore my job.

Social work is the bane of my existence. I wonder if I should have gone into a different field. I'm worn out. I don't know if I'm making a difference.

Most social workers I know love the profession. It is hard work, for sure, but they feel fulfilled to be in a field in which they can make a difference in people's lives and in our society at large. In recent years, with the advent of social media and the ability to express oneself in what seems to some to be a nonthreatening and anonymous way, I have seen a growing number of less-than-positive comments about the profession from within the profession. These comments come from social workers who have fallen out of love with social work, and they are not shy about expressing their disenchantment with what they had hoped would be their dream career. Is burnout on the rise, or are we just hearing more about it in today's digital age? Either way, it seems that something is not quite right with this picture.

Exhausted. Too much to do. Not enough time. Love the profession.

I see posts similar to this regularly on The New Social Worker's page on Facebook. This expresses what I hear from many social workers—that they are feeling overworked, frustrated, and burned out. They are feeling that they are constantly giving and not getting back. They feel unsupported when the work gets too hard and they need someone to listen. At the same time, they love the profession and want to continue to do the work. They don't know what to do with this love-hate tug-of-war with social work. Some will simply leave the profession, thinking this is the only way out. Others will continue to struggle. What has been missing is guidance and support for social workers who are feeling this way.

Good social workers are not immune to the risk of burnout. Maybe you have been feeling this way yourself. Maybe you are wondering what other options you have: find another job, see a therapist, go on a long vacation?

We can start by talking about it. Burnout, compassion fatigue, and vicarious trauma don't have to be endpoints at which time we say, "I'm fed up. I've had enough. I quit social work." We need to talk about this in schools of social work, not to scare students or to say that it is inevitable that they will become burned out but to point out that there are risks *and* that there are things they can do to prevent burnout and to counteract it if and when it happens. We need to be proactive in providing and seeking out the support we as social workers need to be able to work effectively within a profession that presents these risks.

This is where SaraKay Smullens and this book come into the picture. I met SaraKay in 2012, when she proposed to write an article for *The New Social Worker* magazine, where I am the publisher and editor. That article, "What I Wish I Had Known—Burnout and Self-Care in Our Social Work Profession," was published in the Fall 2012 issue. It received the 2013 NASW Media Award for Best Magazine Article. The article received 83,250 page views on The New Social Worker's Web site in the one-year period from October 1, 2013, to September 30, 2014, making it the most read article on the site during that time period. I post the article link on *The New Social Worker's* page on Facebook periodically, and as one example, when it was posted on September 20, 2014, it received 1,317 likes, 162 comments, and 457 shares and reached a total of 95,520 people. As of March 4, 2015, the article itself had received 31,286 "likes." What all of this says to me is that a *lot* of social workers are looking for help with burnout and self-care, and SaraKay's article resonates with them. That article also became the basis for this book.

Burnout and self-care are "hot" topics because they affect so many social workers. Too often, I hear social workers saying that they were not taught enough about burnout, compassion fatigue, vicarious trauma, and countertransference. They feel unprepared for some of the realities of a social work career and perhaps even misled into idealistically believing they will feel fulfilled 100 percent of the time. It is time that we address these issues in our schools of social work and in our agencies. This book gives voice to predictable frustrations in a social worker's experience. It fills a gap, bringing these issues out in the open, where they need to be.

The wonderful thing about this book is that SaraKay joins perspectives of experience and research. She is a social worker who has been there, and she readily shares her insights with her readers. In her 30+ years of experience, she has seen too many good social workers leave the profession, and she really cares about helping them to stay. She also has done thorough research on the topics of burnout and self-care through an extensive review of the existing literature. In addition, she surveyed real social workers for this book and has included their real-life stories. The result is a book that provides clear guidance for social workers, social work students, and those in related fields by not only defining what burnout and self-care are, but also providing real-life examples, suggestions, and questions. Each chapter follows a very clear outline and ends with questions for reflection.

I hope that social workers who are feeling burned out will read this book and discover that there is hope for them to find the love for our profession once again. I hope students and people new to the profession will read this book and learn how to prevent burnout, compassion fatigue, and vicarious trauma in their budding careers and to achieve compassion satisfaction. I encourage you to read and consider the questions at the end of each chapter, and apply them to your own life as a social worker.

With preparation and support, social workers can go beyond the difficult days and thrive in a fulfilling and meaningful profession. They can proactively use self-care to counter the stress of their everyday work. They can once again say, "I love social work," and go home at the end of the day to a more balanced and happy life.

Linda May Grobman, MSW, ACSW, LSW
Publisher/Editor, *The New Social Worker* magazine

Acknowledgments & Reflections

A Letter to Readers

Dear Colleagues and Friends,

Before I begin reading a book, I always study the dedication and acknowledgment pages, if present, for I see these pages as introductions to the writer I will be visiting. Not everyone does this, and of course, it is not necessary for you to do it either. However, if you decide to read these acknowledgments and then complete the book, you will see that these pages are integrated into the message of the book, supporting the importance of reflection and the evidence-based self-care options involving gratitude and journaling.

What I share with you in this section is what I want to say, including some haunting regrets, but I write also to illustrate the self-care emphasis and some of the myriad evidence-based alternatives noted in my book that can lead to fulfillment in a profession that has enormous demands and challenges. Perhaps you will also use what I share in these pages and what follows as a springboard for your own creative approaches to avoiding and addressing burnout. It is my deepest hope that what you will read, in integration with the following pages, will encourage you to identify and create the self-care options that are right for you.

Whereas the researching and writing of this book has taken over two years, the background that led up to its writing has a far longer history. As I recorded my thoughts and experiences in my journal during this period and studied earlier journals, I have been deeply moved, as well as amazed, to recognize a flow and integration of life events and how, even when there are grave losses, disappointments, and great fear, a fulfilling path awaits. You just have to define it. Another truth became apparent: One never knows how much a simple act of kindness may mean to another. There is more that I realized as I remembered: There are so many to be grateful to.

When divorce became necessary in my life in the mid-1970s, I had two very young daughters. The state I had moved to when I married, Pennsylvania, was at that time the only state whose laws had the following barbaric combination: no no-fault divorce, no alimony, and no equitable division of marital property. To be able to afford the necessary psychotherapy to manage the impact of these laws, as well as pay for necessary legal representation, I had to leave a traditional social work setting for private practice. For their representation and support during this period of my life, two attorneys, Albert Momjain and Joseph Weiss, have my enduring thanks. Al Momjain was ably assisted by his young legal colleague, Mary Cushing Doherty, as well as his devoted secretary, Barbara Sonzogni. Each knows my gratitude. Further, I can never adequately thank our beloved friend, Stephen M. Goodman, who became our family lawyer after my second marriage in 1979 and has advised, counseled, and supported our family for decades.

Life has taught me that people see others through a lens developed during their formative years and influenced by how they view their life fulfillment in the present. Friends from youth are more able to see one without this filter. During years that were the most terrifying in my life, the loyalty and kindness of the following friends from earlier chapters in my life remain the most precious of gifts: Bonnie Strauss, Elaine Strauss Rosen, Nancy and James Glazer, Florence Hart, Geraldine and Richard Fox, Marciarose and Jerry Shectack, Joan Frank Goldberg, Carol Hoffman, Donald Joseph, Marilyn Levin, Harriet Schwartz, Agnes Eberling Flaesch, Sonny and Bob Woldow, Ileen and Dr. Michael Shefferman, Margie Levy Lombardo, Willie Mae Washington, Ruth Baldino, Dr. Alan Freedman, Sandy Feinglass Luray, Lorraine Goldenberg Schapiro, Batya Miller, Ethel Miller, Anna Huffington, Florence Cassidy, Mary Barkley, Barbara Brower, Alice Goodman, Ina Orfuss Cohen, Sandy and Mark Laken, Mildred Shifren, Norma Cooper, Sara Shane, Dan Fried, Dr. Barry and Marlene Cooperman and Howard Rubinstein.

I promised myself that as soon as I was able I would once again return to work with clients who had known trauma, intensified by poverty and limited opportunities. This became possible after I remarried, and my small family of three grew into a family of six. In the mid-1990s, Philadelphia District Attorney Lynne Abraham—who at the time of this writing is a candidate for mayor of Philadelphia—offered me the opportunity to work pro bono with select families involved in domestic violence disputes in which actions did not lead to death. In this work I collaborated with Mimi Rose, Esq., the attorney who led the district attorney's family violence unit and who well understood the difference between "a cry for help" and a "criminal mentality."

Through this collaboration, some carefully selected first-time offenders avoided incarceration by agreeing to intensive psychotherapy. In this way, the city could save money as well as help families to grow and change, offering their children hope for the future. I combined this responsibility with my full-time private practice, and in time, other resources within the city also referred pro bono cases.

In addition, the Philadelphia district attorney's office and the Pennsylvania Chapter of the American Jewish Congress supported the formation of the Philadelphia Sabbath of Domestic Peace coalition, which identified clergy as a "missing link" in combating domestic violence. The coalition of professionals, volunteers, and clergy joined to educate clergy of all faiths about the perils of domestic violence, stressing that prayer alone could not stop domestic violence and that if abuse or its threat had taken place, it was dangerous for clergy to meet with partners together. In this effort, I remain grateful to Lynne Abraham and Mimi Rose, as well as Sisters Josephine Kase and the late Marian Dillon, Reverend Debby McKinley, Maureen Rush, William Bergman, Warren Rosen, Dr. Claire Renzetti, Susan Ashbaker, Lynn Marks, Sue Osthoff (and her extraordinary colleagues at the National Clearinghouse for the Defense of Battered Women), Mary Scherf, Claire Ellis, Mary Posner, Gene Dilks, Roberta Hacker (and the dedicated Women In Transition team), Arthur and Abby Ryan, Margot Horwitz, Ruth Laibson, Sara Steele, Charles Ehrlich, Esq., Rabbi Leonard Gordon, Joanne Wszolek, the late Rabbi Gerald Wolpe, and Frank Cervone (and his crucial Support Center for Child Advocates).

The responsibilities of working with families in which parents have known only abuse and deprivation are enormous and cannot be addressed within a traditional nine-to-five framework. To remove an emotional cancer deep within those who have suffered grave deprivation, being there for them and with them in crisis is essential: Through this approach, a "corrective emotional experience" can begin to replace hopelessness and rage, and confidence can begin to replace empty longing and dire feelings of inadequacy.

I am grateful that the clinical approach developed during these years was accepted for publication in two peer-reviewed journals. This approach involved the combination of time-limited group therapy (in which clients described the areas that needed change in their lives through shared written "contracts") with family life education, as well as individual, couple, and family therapy, as indicated.

As I approached my 70th birthday, it became clear that, with the responsibilities of my ongoing clinical practice and writing, I no longer had the energy for work that entailed an around-the-clock commitment. Realizing the number of skilled, committed social workers and those in related professions who left our field due to burnout, I began both to offer workshops concentrating on burnout and self-care and to write about these challenges. It was these workshops and my published work that led to this book.

I am grateful to the former NASW Press acquisition editor, Susan Hills, who contacted me on November 8, 2012, to explore my interest in developing an article I had written in the NASW private practice newsletter, "Self-Care and Avoiding Burnout," into a full-length book. Ms. Hills shepherded me through a book proposal submission (my first) and rejoiced with me when the proposal was accepted. I am equally grateful to the present NASW Press acquisition editor Stella Donovan, who has been available, helpful, and patient throughout the writing and editing of this book. My thanks also to copyeditor Wayson Jones, for his exacting concentration on my manuscript, and to senior editor Sarah Lowman, who has painstakingly and patiently examined every word and thought expressed and has offered invaluable clarification and research guidance. It is also important to thank NASW Press marketing manager, Sharon Fletcher, for her commitment to my book and to gratefully acknowledge the NASW staff member who first encouraged my contribution to social work literature, Stephanie Light Chambers, and the staff members who have encouraged and supported this work, Rochelle Wilder, Yvette Mulkey, Bekki Ow-Ärhus, and Kamilah Omari. Sincere thanks also to my professional colleague and friend, Mila Ruiz Tecala, for her continued support and encouragement of my contribution to social work literature, and to my mentor and friend, Belle Parmet, former director of marriage and family therapy at Carrier Institute, who has consistently urged my research and writing. My gratitude also to Judge Phyllis Beck, and her husband, Dr. Aaron T. Beck, who pioneered the birth of cognitive therapy, for their kindness and support.

I express my deep appreciation and gratitude to Stuart Horwitz for his superb research assistance and his extraordinary editorial and organizational support and guidance, as well as his friendship and that of his wife, psychotherapist Bonnie Kane. This book is but one of several collaborations that would have been impossible without Stuart's friendship, humor, and impeccable talent. Deep appreciation also to my dear friend from graduate school days, Florence Hart, for her generosity and studious, loving attention to my words and thoughts.

It is also essential to thank Linda Grobman, who graciously offered to write the Foreword to this book. My article, "Burnout and Self-Care in Our Social Work Profession: What I Wish I Had Known," appeared in *The New Social Worker* online magazine, which Linda both founded and continues to edit. Other articles I have written have appeared on those pages as well. I am and will remain enormously grateful to Linda for her support and her tireless devotion to our profession.

My devoted thank-yous to my loving friend, the extraordinary, award-winning photojournalist Sharon Wohlmuth Teacher, who despite the recent death of her beloved husband, publisher Larry Teacher, insisted on taking my photograph for this book, as she did my last.

I remain indebted to my mentor and friend, Dr. Mildred Otenasek, who introduced me to President John F. Kennedy at the 1960 Democratic Convention in Los Angeles. President Kennedy was the first person to speak to me about the profession of social work. Through President Kennedy I learned about the Catholic University School of Social Service in Washington, DC, where I was awarded a full scholarship and living allowance stipend. A young woman from an Orthodox Jewish Baltimore family, I was graciously welcomed by the Catholic University faculty, one that included several priests. I have never forgotten these kindnesses, especially those of two advisers and mentors, Grace Llewellyn and Alice Padgett.

After the death of President Kennedy, I married and transferred to the School of Social Work (now the School of Social Policy and Practice) at the University of Pennsylvania, where my husband attended law school. There, I was first introduced to the genius of Otto Rank and was deeply inspired by my professors, Drs. Richard Lodge, Laura Downes, Rosa Wessel, Roland Artigues, and Harold Lewis, as well as my field advisers and mentors Anne Wise, Ruth Scott, Julia Ann Bishop, and Bettie B. Roundtree. After I received my graduate degree, opportunities to study psychoanalytic and psychodynamic theory with Drs. Morris Brody and Eli Marcovitz at the Philadelphia Psychiatric Center, supplemented by consultations with Drs. Stuart Wolfe, David Sachs, Paul Fink, and Stanley Shapiro, have remained invaluable.

There were also cherished teachers and mentors in younger years. Milton (Manny) Velder, my English and homeroom teacher for three years at Baltimore's Garrison Junior High, told me that I could write and urged me to "observe carefully, remember and 'dig within'"—and to not be afraid. My dear teacher could have no way to know that the day I was awarded a writing prize at a graduation ceremony followed some of the most frightening days I had known as a young person, nor could he have known how his words sustained me. It took many years before I developed the confidence to try to believe what my teacher believed about me. At Skidmore College, Professors Henry Galant and Rudolf Sturm also made an enormous difference in my life; and at Goucher College, President Otto Kraushaar and Professors Robert Loevy, Helen Shirley Thomas, and my dear Brownlee Sands Corrin did the same. It has been the deepest of privileges to serve as a Goucher trustee from 2005 through 2014, where I shared trusteeship with dedicated, committed, gifted colleagues and worked with devoted, superb faculty and staff.

My memorabilia from the Kennedy years is divided between the John F. Kennedy Presidential Library and Museum, the Archives of the University of Pennsylvania, and the Special Collections of Goucher College, where I received my undergraduate degree. The bulk of my professional papers are divided between the collections at the University of Pennsylvania and Goucher College. Deep appreciation to Mark Lloyd, director of the Penn Archives; Nancy Magnuson, Goucher College Librarian; and Tara Olivero, Director of Special Collections, for their respectful and painstaking work to make these collections available to students for study and research.

It is also important to recognize my former editors at *The Philadelphia Inquirer*, Tom Wark, the late Bill Stroud, Don Clippinger and my close and dear friend, Sharon Nelton, for their support and guidance during the seven years when I had the privilege of writing a Sunday column for Philadelphia's brave Pulitzer Prize-winning hometown newspaper. Through this column, intended to support and inform, not entertain, my editors offered a unique professional responsibility to respond in depth to one letter each Sunday. I will remain grateful for their support in addressing the suffering brought on by Pennsylvania's brutal and barbaric divorce laws, as they existed at the time. Although at the column conclusion it was stated that I could not respond personally to the volume of mail received, whenever a letter involved a problem that could be addressed in a meaningful way (these were the days before e-mail communication), I either wrote or telephoned the writer.

Most of us in our professional lives will, in time, look back on errors with deep regret but also see them as opportunities to learn and improve. The oversight I will describe involved a lapse in response to an urgent letter: Following my divorce and a period as a single parent, I remarried in 1979, and two families of three worked together to form a new family. During this time of adjustment for all six of us, I received a long, handwritten letter that deserved an immediate response. The letter was from a young teenager who blamed herself for the death of someone she loved dearly. I well remember feeling the anguish of the young writer as I placed her letter on my desk (or so I believed), planning to respond as soon as I had a break in my day. The letter, which provided important contact information, should have been placed in a protected drawer for confidential material immediately, for when I returned to my desk, it was nowhere to be found. I looked and looked and repeatedly asked family members if they had seen it, but it just seemed to vanish. Even now, many years later, if I come across an unusual file, I immediately look through it carefully, hoping to find the lost letter. I have often hoped that the letter writer and my path could somehow cross, that her life has moved forward positively, and that I would have the opportunity to apologize.

Following the end of this column, I was invited to begin writing in an entirely different analytical format. This new and exciting opportunity involved writing op-ed and commentary pieces that examined political and societal events and issues through a psychosocial prism. This work was edited by the brilliant Shakespearian scholar and poet John Timpane at *The Philadelphia Inquirer* and the exceptional, vital, and devoted newspaper editor at *The Philadelphia Daily News*, Michael Schefer. To have been published at the *Inquirer* during the leadership of the incomparable editor and Pulitzer Prize winner William K. Marimow has been the deepest of privileges.

My deep gratitude also to Dan Rottenberg, who edited and published my work when he led what is now the *The Philadelphia Weekly* and then continued to publish it in the Philadelphia gem devoted to the excellent, diverse art world in Philadelphia, the *Broad Street Review*, which he founded. It is also important to thank my close friend, the best-selling author and editor Gloria Hochman, for the writing opportunities and guidance she has so very generously provided through the years and to acknowledge the ever-present personal and professional support of broadcast journalist and filmmaker Bonnie Strauss and broadcast pioneer Marciarose Shestack. I am also grateful to Dan Geddes, the brave editor of *The Satirist* (published in Amsterdam), for printing my satire and for telling me that one of my blogs he found made him laugh, something that social workers do not often hear, and to the gifted writer and editor Leslie Bennetts, whom I was fortunate to meet when my children were very young.

It is my privilege to thank Arianna Huffington, who invited me to blog for *The Huffington Post*, and I would like to share a special reflection involving our meeting. When I worked at the Democratic Convention in 1960, I was in a crowded room, knowing no one, when Eleanor Roosevelt entered. She stopped when she was about to pass me (because she saw I was a student) and offered her hand as she said: "Hello, I'm Eleanor Roosevelt (as if I did not know!). Tell me about you." Fast forward to another crowded gathering several years ago, when I was once again standing alone: Arianna Huffington was about to pass me but stopped, extending her hand with the precise greeting of so many years before: "Hello, I'm Arianna Huffington (as if I did not know!). Tell me about you." From this conversation, the invitation to blog for *The Huffington Post* was offered. It is important to note that no one has done more to educate the general public about the importance of self-care than Arianna. It is a privilege to be on her pages with the committed care of her astute editorial staff and blog team. Special thanks to executive blog editor Stuart Whatley.

Thanks also to my editor at *Your Tango*, Melanie Gorman, whose skill, vision, and commitment to the direction and satisfaction in life and love make contributing to *Your Tango* a pleasure. It is also important to note the help, constancy, and friendship of Trisha Torrey who developed my first web page, so necessary when my second book was published. Trisha continued as my webmaster long after she began her burgeoning career as a health care advocate. I am deeply appreciative also of the help, constancy, and friendship of Michelle Taglialatela and Eric Crawford, who are developing and will care for my new Web page.

Thank you also to my dear friend and the editor of my first book, Laurie Graham. Laurie is the most gifted of writers and editors, and her friendship remains invaluable. It is not possible to put into words the difference that she and the president of Scribner's Book Companies, Franklyn L. Rodgers (known as Buck to those who met him during his years at the University of Pennsylvania, and Lee to most who met him through the publishing world), have made in my life. I will always remain grateful to the late Robbin Reynolds, who believed in my writing and brought my manuscript to the attention of Laurie and Scribner's, as well as the late Carl Brandt, who also supported and nurtured my writing. It is also important to thank an enduring friend, Stephen H. Wells, PhD, Esq., for introducing Robbin to my writing, as well as for his unforgettable generosity and confidence in my clinical skill and creative abilities.

Gratitude also to New Horizon Press and its Wakefield publisher, Dr. Joan S. Dunphy. Dr. Dunphy recognized the importance of codifying cycles of emotional abuse as separate and distinct from physical and sexual abuse, understanding that although emotional abuse is always part of physical and sexual violence, its cycles and patterns can exist independently. My thanks also to Elaine Jean Cooper, PhD, for her guidance in the publication of a paper devoted to this topic, "The Codification and Treatment of Emotional Abuse in Structured Group Therapy" in the *International Journal of Group Psychotherapy*, as well as to the journal editor, Les R. Greene PhD, now President of the American Group Psychotherapy Association, and training psychoanalyst David Sachs, MD. The counsel and contributions of each has been invaluable. Also indispensable has been the generous communication with Dr. Jerome C. Wakefield, professor of social work at the NYU Silver School, regarding my writing on the disconnect between psychiatric research and clinical social work practice and my expressed disappointment that social worker input was nonexistent in final decisions regarding diagnostic evaluations in the DSM-5.

Enduring thanks also to Blanche Schlessinger, my literary agent and devoted friend, for her crucial support and patient guidance from the moment we met.

It is also essential to thank my friend, the enormously gifted writer and editor Nancy Steele, who worked with me to transform well over one thousand pages of thought, reflection, and research into the manuscript submitted to New Horizon Press. Unquestionably, without Blanche and Nancy, my second book would never have been accepted for publication.

My sincere thanks to Dawn Cassidy, our committed and caring director of education for the National Council on Family Relations. Dawn oversees the certification process of the National Council on Family Relations' family life educators, whose tireless contributions to evidence-based family life education is invaluable.

I also want to note some of the many professional presentations that I attended in the last few years. The research shared by my fellow social workers was significant, meaningful, and uplifting to me as I sought resources to encourage social work students and professionals. These presentations include: Carol Tosone, PhD, "When the Professional Is Personal: Trauma and Its Impact on the Clinician," December 2013, sponsored by the Pennsylvania Society of Clinical Social Work; Phyllis Black, PhD, and Michael Jeffrey, LCSW, "Social Workers Come With Baggage: Past and Recent Psychosocial Trauma," and Mark Shaffer, LCSW, "Blending the Arts of Self-Compassion and Self-Care," October 2013, NASW-PA Annual Conference; Rhegina Sinozich, LCSW-C, "The Power of Happiness: Positive Psychology and Its Implications for Treatment," Eva Forde, MSSW, "Rich Social Worker: Making the Case for More Money and Personal Fulfillment in Social Work," Pantea Rahimian, LCSW, "An Exploratory Study Addressing the Stress and Self Care Levels of Social Work Graduate Students," Amber Dion, MSW, "Trauma and Addictions: Balancing Indigenous and Western Healing Practices," Susan Pease Banitt, LCSW, "Trauma and the HPA Axis: Emerging Holistic Paradigms for Social Work and Psychotherapy," Ellen Siegel, LCSW, "21st Century Call to Our High Functioning: The Inner Self Care Model," Violet Cox-Wingo, LISW-S, "Compassion Fatigue: "I Am Dancing As Fast As I Can"; Linda Butler, MSW, "Grant Seeking: Best Practices and Leadership," Reeta Wolfsohn, CMSW, "Financial Social Work: Playing a Role in Economic and Social Justice," July 2014, NASW National Conference; social psychologist Clark McCauley, PhD, "The Psychology of Terrorism and Mass Murder," a Philadelphia community lecture.

I will remain indebted to over 200 social workers who generously used their limited personal time to complete the questionnaires vital for this book. I am grateful to the people and resources that published my request for their participation: Linda Grobman and *The New Social Worker*; Deborah Shain, Patricia Isakowitz, Laura Favin, and Kathy Biedler, each so vital to social work through steadfast contributions to the superb *Pennsylvania Society for Clinical Social*

Work and beyond; Ron Simon, Mike Jeffrey, and Tara Breitsprecher, each crucial to NASW-PA; Marci Kennal, LCSW, former director of the Anne Arundel County Department of Social Services; Joseph Porter at Skidmore College, where I spent my first two years of undergraduate work; and my good friend, Nadina Deigh, associate dean for institution advancement at my graduate school alma mater, the University of Pennsylvania School of Social Policy and Practice (formerly the University of Pennsylvania School of Social Work). I also thank dean of students and director of the Penn DSW program, Dr. Lina Hartocollis, for her generous review and support of my manuscript and both Lina and Professor Ram Cnaan for their years of validation of my writing and social work commitments. Grateful thanks to Marie and Joseph Field for making it possible to establish the Field Center, an adjunct of my alma mater, which brings together University of Pennsylvania resources to address the needs of our most vulnerable children and families.

If one receives the extraordinary gift of a long, full life, the loss of those cherished is inevitable. Close friends in my life are "chosen family," and the following loyal friends and family members, who made an enormous difference in my life and the lives of my family, will continue to live in my heart: Elaine Strauss Rosen, Judge Edward Becker, Dina Wind, Jerome Shestack, Esq., Marlene Cooperman, Esq., Jeanette Kean, Rabbi Uri Miller, Benjamin Strauss, Howard Koerpel, Dr. Mildred Otenasek, Milton (Manny) Velder, Lucille and Dr. Woodrow Savacol, Frances and Dr. Thomas Mervine, Ruth Zar, Rena Rubell, Lee Friedman, William (Bill) Stroud, Dr. Warren Goldburgh, Carter Buller, Esq., Dorothy Rubin, Donald J. Goldberg, Esq., Lenora Berson, Valla and Gus Amsterdam, Dr. Rhoda Dorsey, Betsy and Ed Meyer, Romayne Sachs, Daniel B. Allanoff, Anne Hunt, Mary Mallie, Dorothy Orfuss Stein, Beatrice Sherman, Mildred Shifren, Marjorie Schwartz, Sue-Ellen Streen, Archie Perlmutter, Jennie Coast, Lee Friedman, Larry Teacher, Ernesta Ballard, Irene Scherr, Dr. Stuart First, Dr. Hugh Rosen, Dr. Paul Fink, Dr. Michael Shefferman, Irv Borowsky, Dr. Benjamin Bacarach, Richard Woldow, Wesley Emmons, Stuart Young, Esq., Archie Perlmutter, Senator Arlen Specter, Leonard Brown, Eileen and Bill Brown, Judy Feldman, Pat Guy, Lenore Schwartz. Dr. Jerry Cotler, Otto Sperr, Wesley Emmons, Dr. Joe Rodgers, Stan Hochman, and my new friend, Eric Porter; and cherished grandparents, Kate Sherman (and her beloved sister, Anna Goodman) and Sol Orfuss, and deeply missed parents, Charlotte and Charles Sherman, whom I speak of later; and my mother's beloved sister and brother-in-law, who were also dear to me, Edna and Robert Obeck.

This book addresses the emotional toll of the real-life horror social workers and those in related fields face with our clients on a day-to-day basis. Images of the cruelty and suffering we see haunt us, and even when we take very good care of ourselves, visions may appear, seemingly out of nowhere, often during happy and fulfilling times. And sometimes, in the quiet of the night, there are tears.

I will never forget the experience I had as a young social worker when a child I was responsible for died of neglect and abuse: My six-year-old client, who had cerebral palsy, was being starved and was confined to her crib in a dark and dirty room. I immediately petitioned for her removal from her home and parents, but although the evidence was clear, the judge hearing our case sent her home, where she died.

It is impossible for social workers, educators, and mental health professionals to be immune to these experiences or to forget them. But in reflection, as I write now, I well understand that these memories are as they should be. We should *not* forget. Remembering is a sign of humanity, and our memories should be used to propel us to keep on working as hard as we can to support and protect the most vulnerable among us for as long as we can.

Even our closest friends usually have no idea of the differences they make as they call to say hello, fill us in on their lives, ask about us and our loved ones, and suggest sharing a meal, seeing a film, or simply taking a walk. As you will read, social workers do not usually tell our friends, or even our family members, about our days, for often there are no words. I hope in my own way I have thanked friends and colleagues whose caring and support, expressed in myriad ways, have been invaluable, even when time, distance, and responsibilities in our lives do not allow frequent contact. Quality, trusting connections and kindness, even when time is limited, are an essential part of the self-care opportunities addressed in this text.

There are many whose names follow with whom I am not in touch on a regular basis but who have offered far more than I believe they realize. Heartfelt, enduring thanks to Bonnie Strauss Gould and Dr. Roger Gould, Dr. Janis and Steve Goodman, Barbara and Robert Tiffany, Marciarose Shestack, Marilyn and Dr. Irwin Scher, Florence and Peter Hart, Dr. Jerry (Yoram) Wind, Cintra and Buck Rodgers, Nancy and Jim Steele, Judy Friedman, Marie and Joe Field, Jaimie and David Field, Stacey Spector and Ira Brind, Ellen Singer Coleman and Michael Coleman, Jackie Cooperman and Jason Shrednick and Livia, Dr. José Bowen, Jennifer Fox, Dov Shestack, Portia Iversen and Jonathan Shestack, Jennifer Shestack, Ruth and Dr. Peter Laibson, Toby Meyer, Sally and Mo Barron, Margot and Ellis Horwitz, Kathy and Ken LaMotte, Harriet and Dr. Gene Abroms, Judy and Maurie Kaplow, Libby Horwitz and Dr. Bert Blender, Sharon Wohlmuth and Larry Teacher, Peppy Fink, Agnes Eberling Flaesch, Pam and Dr. Alan Schreiber, Lee Alter, Paula Cramer and Warren Ladden, Leona and Nelson Shanks, Ellen Emmons, Barbara Lutz, Kathy Ahern, Gwen Goodman, Mary Montague, Jean and Dr. Tom Nasca, Ellen and Bob Seltzer, Dr. Judy

Finkle, Linda Hing, Karen and Doug Peters, David and Ligia Slovak, Susan and Dr. Roger Daniels, Judge Flora Becker, Joyce and Carl Norden, Dr. Mallory Eisenman, Nancy Colbaugh, Dr. Dana and Maria Kaminstein, Marilyn Lager, Carol Saline and Paul Rathblott, Florence Cotler, Julie Curson, Bunny Glick, Kiki Hughes, Tony Young, Bojan Spassoff, Stephanie Wolf Spassoff, Ellen Bonett, Caro Rock, Sue Rock (and the Rock School family), Tony Young, Judge Phyllis Beck, Judith Hyman, Carol Jacques, Dr. Basil Snyman, Dr. Pauline Park and Jack Panich, Nancy Jacobsen, Laurie Borowsky, Dr. Faith Bethelard, Joan and Victor Johnson, Janice Levin, Judy and Dr. George Wohreich, Miriam Passarello, Manny Velder and his Garrison 215 loyalists, Josephine Mandeville, Mary Duden, Jo Ann Buller, Nancy and Steve Smith, Sharon and Dr. Robert Strochak, Nancy Colbaugh, Dr. Ben and Ginny Kendall, Elaine Wanicur and Ed Levy, Paula Brown, Ellen Brown, Ruth and Sheldon Weinstein, Sally and Steve Herman, Kate Morro, Lynn Fisher and Lee Compton, Ruth and Jay Lenrow, Toby Werthheim, Robert Hazzon, Adele and Dr. Bert Greenspan, Gloria and Stan Hochman, Judith Hyman, Kevin Kim, Elly Bulova, Stephanie and Roland Kallen, Claudia Horwitz, Dr. Lorraine King, Dr. William Tasman, Dr. Paul Nyirjesy, Cynthia Bayer, Dr. George Valco, Janet Burnham, Dr. Maryanne Ruby, Estelle Koerpel (and Susan and Iris), Florence Cotler, Rose Greco, Madeleine Barnes, Alan Biddle, Suzanne and Ralph Roberts, Dr. Ed Ruby, Elizabeth Hart, Lisa Herz, Dr. Barbara Porges, April K. Ferry, Lucy Clemens, Peter Amobei, Mary Ewen, Drew McKeown. Renee Rector, Kim Morgan, Ralph Davies, Lira Lee Cohen, Sandy Steinberg Harris, Nancy and Will Braveman, Evelyn Malcohm, HattieRuth Reese, Norma Cooper, Willie Mae Washington, Denise Highsmith, Joy and Dr. Aaron Bannett, Adrienne Rodgers, Margie David, Pam Rodgers, Melissa Coleman, Chris Ramsey, Cecile and Eugene Block, Zola Bryen, Esther Rahavi and Jerry Kellner, Paula and Ellen Brown, Ruth Septee, Dr. David Stein, Mary McMonigle, Marianne Anthony, Barbara and Ed Silver, Lonnie and Murray Levin, Marion and Dr. Richard Taxin, Dr. Bettyruth Walter, Dr. Ed Guy, Len Feldman, Kathy Feldman, Ellen and Bill Alesker, Elaine and Dr. Malcolm Eckert, Barbara Freed and Alan Middleman, Joy Hockman and Jack Silverberg, Rosalie Matzkin, Linda Rebstock, Jamie Stroud, Tracey Sutton, Cathy Hozack, Ann Hozack, Dr. Kenneth and Rochelle Laudenbach, Debbie Yaniko-Morris, Amanda Cerini, Christine Marucci, Therese Obringer, Elaine Levitt Gershman, Hilary Jay, Karen and Doug Peters, Alice and Richard Mandel, Nancy and James Weiss, Ellen Yin, Dr. Paul and Joan Bucker, Dr. William and Dee Bleumle, Leanne and Joe Sebastianelli, Marty and Walter Rosen, Lori Ross, Sally Ross, Glenn St. Coeur, Garth Weldon, Janice and Percy Moore, Julie Curson, Lynne Kreis, Andrea Frey, Simo Lazizi, Tim Hill, Linda Rebstock, Bill and Adrienne Cramer, Jackie Moore, Dov and his Tawes family, Alex Wood, Pat and Sam Holt, Toby Rosen Holzer, Nancy and Larry Abrams, Joan Shepp and her Chestnut Street family, Jan and Doug Cox, Nancy and Dr. Walter Herman, Barbara and Ed Silver, Dr. Miriam Spector, Carol Jacques, Joanne Cunningham, Linda Berman, Marci Reudiger, Lenore Rose, Dr. Judith Sills, Fusako Yokobori, Hope Broker, Judy Leib, Ruth Hirshey, Carol Parks Weis, Dr. Howard and Barbara First, Jennifer Heller and Lou Lappen, Joe Canuso and Trish Kelly, Mary Gill, Jody Buonanno Shue, Helen Dulin, Bill Moy, Jessica McCoach, Joan Goldburgh, Dr. Pat Kennedy, Kim and Roger Leibowitz, Drs. David Shefferman and Nereida Segura-Rico, Scott and Ilissa Shefferman, Vlada Rouseff, Nancy Blum, Patty and Donald Freed, Norman Berson, Dr. Ruth Perlmutter, Dr. Phyllis Fischer (and the Philadelphia Jewish Film Festival family), Rabbi Richard and Diane Steinbrink Melissa Coleman, Tina and Frank Rutan, Dr. Anthony DiMarino, Diane Pickering, Dr. Linda Himmelberger, Sheila Hamersky, Baziah Young, Irene and David Hornstein, Francine Roberts, and the Warwick-Radisson family; Patricia Batza, Percy and Janice Moore, Janet Wiley, Debbie Burton, Gigi Greenfield, Shelly Hillebrand, Lillian Johnson, Reverend Cynthia Terry, Cori Tyner, Sylvia Hesson, Kate Pipkin, Judy Woods, Gigi Greenfield, Bonnie Fishpaw, Nancy Turner, Kevin Krakower, Dr. Arthur and Suzanne Schless, Dee Josephs, Drs. Ann Eichen and Andrew Smolar, Beverly Lewis Wilson, Allison Feinstein Cohen, Nancy Goldy, Drs. Marianne Ruby and Gary Emmett.

It is important also to recognize an unusually dynamic friendship experience that has endured for well over a decade: A group of men and women who lived in various neighborhoods in downtown Philadelphia (most of us had never laid eyes on each other!) were invited by an indomitable leader, the late Valla Amsterdam, and two who were very involved in Philadelphia's burgeoning cultural scene, the late Mae Richard and Ruth Lief Miller, to meet together on the first Sunday afternoon of every month to talk and share. Our group adopted the name "Let's Talk." Sometimes speakers were invited; sometimes group members spoke and led a discussion; and sometimes the group members spoke among themselves. Our group disbanded as our children left home, and we wanted to be freer to plan unscheduled weekends. But we "reunion" with regularity whenever possible, now good friends who shared and continue to share important moments and transitions. In addition to my husband and me, those who participated in this very special experience demonstrated the essence of self-care through constancy, availability, and thoughtful conversation: the late Valla and Gus Amerstam, Barbara and Robert Tiffany, Laurie Wagman and the late Irv Borowsky, Judith Dean and James Crawford, the late

Mae and the late Howard Richard, Susan Davidson and John V. R. Bull, the late Amy Galfand, Judith and the late Lee Friedman, Caroline Simon, Sylvia and Al Glassman, Lou Gambaccini, Ruth Leif Miller, Doris and Leo Levin, Linda Lee Alter, Carol Saline and Paul Rathblott, the late Evelyn Feldman Rock and the late Eli Rock, Diane and the late Bob Rossheim, Leah and the late Jussi Saukkonen, and Seymour Mednick.

I wish my exquisite and extraordinarily sensitive and perceptive mother and highly intelligent father, Charlotte and Charles Sherman, had been offered just a fraction of my many opportunities. I have never forgotten the kindnesses of members of my extended family, named earlier, who did all they could to care for me during the years, from ages three to almost seven, when I did not live with my mother. I wish I had the skill to do justice to the generosity of my neighbors on Oswego Avenue, in Baltimore's Lower Park Heights area, who cared for me during this period, often from early morning until evening, treating me as if I were one of their own. (Ours was the neighborhood brought to life in Barry Levinson's 1990 film, *Avalon,* which was the name of our local "movie house.") However, I feel I must try to express my gratitude to them: they owed me nothing, yet gave me so much. Please note: In the following reminiscences, the names Cassie and Marybeth replace actual names, and identifying materials involving them are altered. The others, of blessed memory (other than two unnamed teachers, remembered not at all blessedly), are recollections of real people who, along with Cassie and Marybeth, offered love, safety, and kindness to a frightened child.

Josephine O'Neill, whom I called "Miss Josephine" (so did everyone else, except for the two unmarried brothers who lived with her and called her Josie), told me endless stories as we sat on her porch sipping lemonade (actually she sipped and I gulped) or inside in cold weather drinking hot chocolate. (Miss Josephine always kept her little finger raised while drinking because "that's what ladies do.") Even more important, she showed me the wondrous contents of her jewelry box, describing in detail what each "gentleman suitor" had given her, and she gave me a brooch, which I cherish to this day.

Mr. and Mrs. Charlie, who owned the corner "grocery-everything else" store (and lived above it), saved candy for me daily. When our neighbor, Cassie, who in the intense city heat of summer would give me a midday bath when she bathed her daughter, Mrs. Charlie would take a work break and join us, gossiping with Cassie as the two of them drank scalding tea in the steamy bathroom, explaining that it helped them to cool down. One summer, Cassie had a miscarriage, and Mrs. Charlie and I were no longer invited to her home. Cassie sat on her porch alone, motionless, for weeks, as I heard neighbors whisper among themselves that Cassie "lost her baby." One day as I ate my candy, I told Mrs.

Charlie that I did not understand how someone lost her baby. Mrs. Charlie explained that the baby had not been born, which I still did not understand, and she gave me a sympathy card. Although Mrs. Charlie could write only Yiddish, she tried hard to help me to sign the card, and that evening I slipped it under Cassie's front door. I remember two versions of what happened next: In one, Cassie smiled faintly and nodded to me from her porch. In another, I never saw her again. Soon after, Cassie moved away, and I agonized that my card had upset her even more.

Mildred Shifren often took me to the Avalon to see movies and on her weekly trips to the library. Mildred always made sure she had the latest bestseller in hand, and she explained all plots to me in intimate detail; she also told me the "facts of life," and though I didn't understand a word, I nodded in rapt attention, thrilled that she found me so grown up. Mildred loved her husband Louie a lot, but I think he drove a cab and was not home much, so she had lots of time for their precious daughter Lois and for me. I often braided Lois's hair, and she named her doll SaraKay. Mildred, Louie, and Lois lived with Mildred's parents, Mr. and Mrs. Gus Goldstein, who gave me many photographs of their "lost family from the old country" to place in an album. This project took weeks. I used scotch tape, a gift from Mr. and Mrs. Charlie, and did a very clumsy job, ruining some of the photos with the tape, yet the Goldsteins, Mildred, and Lois spent hours pouring over the photos, telling me that I had given them a home, and thanking me repeatedly. Mr. Goldstein drank spilled coffee from his saucer, something that my Bubbie, my paternal grandmother, said only pigs did. Bubbie explained, "Maybe it was OK in the 'old country,' but not in the 'new' one"; she made me promise never, ever to do "*such a thing.*" One evening while having supper with Mr. and Mrs. Goldstein, Mr. Goldstein picked up his saucer and slurped the remaining coffee, I immediately told him he was acting like a pig. Both Mr. and Mrs. Goldstein thought this hilarious and roared with laughter. I concluded that being honest was a good thing.

Mr. and Mrs. Jolson—who, everyone said, were related to the world's greatest entertainer, Al Jolson—had two beautiful young adult daughters, Wilma and Beverly, each living away from home. Mrs. Jolson would spend hours reading to me on weekend afternoons, as her husband carefully studied the newspapers. Whereas Mr. Goldstein had his supper in his undershirt, Mr. Jolson always wore a suit and tie. He never drank his coffee from a saucer, and Mrs. Jolson always put on a lovely dress for dinner. I used to love to watch her fix her hair and apply makeup before her large Deco mirror, part of her bedroom dressing table. Her pot roast was scrumptious.

The beautiful teenager, Marybeth, an only child, took me to fairs sponsored by her church and showed me her favorite movie magazines. But I found her parents to be cold, unwelcoming, even frightening, and I only joined Marybeth inside her home if she insisted. The last time I visited, I heard her parents pretend to whisper about me, Jewish people, and others. It was obvious that they wanted me to hear them, even though they knew I would not understand their words. At this time in Baltimore, various neighborhoods, facilities, and restaurants had signs that read: "Restricted: No Jews, Negroes, or Dogs"; restrooms and public drinking fountains were segregated, and black people rode in the back of all public transportation. Later, I realized that what I heard from my friend's parents was their wish that Oswego Avenue also had a "Restricted" sign.

When Miss Josephine died, her brothers, weeping uncontrollably, took me inside their home to visit with her. "Our Josie will see you from heaven paying your respects," they explained, each taking one of my hands. Miss Josephine, her long ever-blond hair cascading down her shoulders, wore a light blue lace dress and her favorite "suitor" jewelry. To me, she looked at peace and truly beautiful; and though frightened by seeing a person who was dead, I remember believing that her anguished brothers told me the truth—from somewhere above, my dear Miss Josephine was glad I was there.

On my favorite evenings, Pop, my maternal grandfather, read *War and Peace* and *Anna Karenina* to me, or we listened to *The Lone Ranger* on the radio. (The time was 7:30 P.M., and I think the day was Monday, but I am not sure.) Pop walked me to my first day in kindergarten, eliciting a promise that I would always be a good student. I was to let him down miserably: I couldn't sing or draw, and because of this, my two kindergarten teachers kept me inside during every recess to practice scales and drawing (I was hopeless), along with those who were punished for wetting their pants. During this period of humiliation, my grandfather died. For days I looked for him everywhere, even under his house, where my mother found me one evening. She told me that as Pop was dying, he felt he was being choked and said, "That child is tickling me to death." My mother's words clinched my deepest fear: I became sure that my disgraceful failure during my first experience as a student had killed my beloved Pop.

When my mother temporarily recovered and we left Oswego Avenue for Baltimore's suburban Mount Washington, I missed everyone (but my teachers and Marybeth's parents) horribly. However, on my first day at Mount Washington Elementary School, everything changed. On this day my teacher, Miss Ethel Miller, asked each in our class to draw a picture. Then she tested our singing voices. (We sang "Silent Night.") The next day, when I fearfully arrived at school, expecting to once again experience rejection, shame, and humiliation, I found my picture (of a train) with others placed above the backboard. Further, Miss Miller invited me to be the only member of the glee club who did not sing, but instead introduced the songs. She explained that if I wished, after each introduction, I could stand with the others. As they sang, she suggested that I move my lips, which I did.

Now to the most important part of my very small corner of our very vast world: my family. Everything changed in my life when I met my husband, Stanton Smullens, on January 3, 1979. It was as if we had been looking for each other always. Now, over 35 years after our marriage, even more deeply in love, it becomes harder and harder to remember a time in our adult lives when we have not been together. I will always remain grateful to Stan's medical colleague at Jefferson Hospital, the late Warren Goldburgh, who introduced us. I often told Warren that few cardiologists understood the human heart as well as he did. In addition, I will remain ever grateful for Stan's invaluable availability to discuss the issues in this book, as well as his research support and direction and his deeply appreciated generosity regarding the countless hours of work necessary for its completion. Much of this work occurred during the precious and limited hours that our professional responsibilities would have allowed us to be together. Attention also must be paid to my husband's extraordinary patience during the hours between midnight and 5 A.M., when my computer often seemed to have a mind of its own, including the time it began erasing everything. Stan has gone from micro to macro medicine and is now an administrator; and I have appreciated his kind spirit during these times, even when thoroughly exasperated: "Don't worry," he would tell me (sometimes after a rather loud, "What the hell?"), "I am a surgeon, and surgeons can always get back to sleep." (If, as you read, you note a contradiction between the hours that I often worked on the book and the necessity for sleep stressed as an important aspect of self-care, you are a careful reader. Like you, I am a social worker with a complex workday and a private life that is important to me, but writing has also become exceedingly important to me; nights for me are a quiet, peaceful time to concentrate. Right now you could pack for a full weekend in the bags under my eyes, but this, I swear, is a time-limited situation!)

Before Stan, the happiest events in my life were the births of my daughters, Elisabeth and Kathyanne. My first book is dedicated to them. My marriage to Stan brought two more wondrous children to love, Liz and Doug. My husband and I were each determined to do all we could to ease the pain our past mistakes had brought our children. Within moments of our first hellos, there was an immediate connection between the six of us, and that is when the real work of creating a trusting family began. This work has continued as our family has grown. Ever with us has been the beloved memory of Stan's oldest child, Jonathan, who died at age 17, several months before his father and I met.

Stan's and my children are now married to partners who have brought great joy to our lives: deepest love to Elisabeth and Russ LaMotte, Liz and Andreas Brass, Kathyanne and Adam Schess, and Deborah Block and Douglas Smullens. We are proud and respectful of you each, all you have brought to each other and your families, and your individual professional commitments and extremely hard work. We are also deeply grateful for the kindness and respect you show us.

Stan and I are enormously thankful for the gifts of our grandchildren: Charlotte Rose, Amelia, Lucy, Stella, Parker, Josh, Jordana, and Jacov. Each is so special in unique ways: We love you dearly and deeply and thank your parents for their generosity in allowing us to have special time with you; and we thank you for your precious friendship and kindnesses to us. Also, I would be enormously remiss if I did not mention our wonderful granddog, Abe. And I have to confess that I was always a cat person until Abe came into my life.

I also thank my clients, who, through decades, have continued to inspire me with their bravery and determination. And I thank those of you I join in devotion and commitment to our work and those we are privileged to serve. I hope these pages will inform and hold meaning for you. Despite all of the challenges noted, I cannot imagine a greater honor or privilege than to be present with our clients as they work toward their hopes and dreams and the opportunities they deserve.

To be continued,

SaraKay Smullens
April 10, 2015

Introduction

What I Wish I Had Known

The training to become a social worker is arduous, demanding, and complex. My concentration was clinical social work, which, during my graduate education, was known as casework. I well remember studying my basic curriculum; taking more electives than were required; receiving excellent supervision of my clinical work with individuals, couples, families, and groups; and, before it was required, taking many continuing education classes.

I learned a great deal, but what it seemed that no one shared with me during these years, or seemed to discuss among themselves, was the sheer exhaustion experienced in every concentration of social work as we do our very best to meet our clients' needs day after day, year after year. When one of my deeply trusted supervisors died, and I met his wife for the first time, she told me that sometimes he would return home too exhausted to even speak and that a frequent statement she heard from a man who obviously treasured his clinical work, teaching, and writing was: "They feel better, but I surely do not." How well I understood this feeling, I thought. How well so many in our field must understand this feeling. And yet many of us lack the attendant knowledge that can assess and direct this feeling, which is called "burnout" in the literature— or knowledge of the necessary practices to heal and soothe ourselves, which are collectively known as "self-care." What I have learned over the years is the necessity of addressing this complicated exhaustion before the feeling of depletion leads to dysfunction or more serious disintegration. With this in mind, I share the precise information that I wish I had known about burnout and self-care in the early years of my work.

The term "burnout" was first applied by Freudenberger (1974) to describe what happens when a practitioner becomes increasingly "inoperative." According to Freudenberger (1975), this progressive state of inoperability can take many different forms, from simple rigidity, in which "the person becomes 'closed' to any input" (p. 79) to an increased resignation, irritability, and quickness to anger. As burnout worsens, however, its effects turn more serious. An individual may become paranoid or self-medicate with legal or illegal substances. Eventually, a social worker afflicted with burnout may leave a promising career that he or she has worked very hard to attain or be removed from a position by a forced resignation or firing.

Various studies have reported figures of moderate burnout on the part of social workers ranging from 47 percent (Maslach, Jackson, & Leiter, 1996) to as high as 71 percent (Martin & Schinke, 1998). The research accompanying these studies points to a direct correlation between burnout and the desire to leave one's job (Lloyd, King, & Chenoweth, 2002). Gibson, McGrath, and Reid (1989) found that 73 percent of respondents had thought of leaving social work at some point. Yet even with the signs of burnout all around us, social workers may still not pay full attention to the reality of that possibility until suddenly everything seems overwhelming. At such times, we may lack the knowledge of what is transpiring or the critical faculties to assess our experience objectively that will enable us to take proper measures to restore balance to our lives. To explore and understand the phenomenon of burnout before it is too late, researchers have found it useful to introduce several components of the term or attendant syndromes; in this work, I have made use of three of them specifically: compassion fatigue, countertransference, and vicarious trauma.

Just as burnout is associated with personal and professional factors, adjustment to those factors prevents future or further burnout from occurring. Further, it can reverse burnout that has occurred. In other words, there is a cure for burnout; not a permanent cure, or a cure-all, but a process that can restore balance in our personal and professional lives. That cure is self-care, a practice that can be actively committed to in four arenas: the professional, including organizational, supervisory, and peer strategies; the personal, including the psychological, emotional, and religious/spiritual dimensions; the social, including one's partner, immediate family, and circle of friends and acquaintances; and the physical, the care of one's own body.

Lately, increased attention has been given to the concept of self-care, the balancing activities in which social workers can engage to preserve personal longevity and happiness, their relationships, and their careers. These activities span a wide range and can include receiving support from mentors or a peer group, the importance of relaxation (including vacations), the pursuit of personal hobbies and interests, and the need to balance wellness with one's professional life. By engaging in self-care, we can assert our right to be well and reintroduce our own needs into the equation. Self-care is not merely one of those "nice-to-haves": Among the many consequences of burnout is poor-quality client care. Organizations thus must take note: We cannot simply give lip service to self-care and then get social workers back on a demanding tread-mill without compromising client care and staff well-being.

In this book, you will find the examination of burnout and self-care communicated through four distinct dimensions. First, there is the research; since the concept of burnout was first introduced by Freudenberger, there have been scores of important thinkers engaged in an intensive qualitative and quantitative discussion of the aspects of burnout and self-care. The second dimension comes from a qualitative case study I have conducted over the past two years: Drawing from over 200 prospective candidates, 40 social workers were selected to complete an anonymous, extensive questionnaire. Their responses pointed to the exact problems of burnout and blessings of self-care in a unique way, and because of their efforts, we are able to hear authentic voices of those on the front lines of social work and mental health practice. In addition, there are the case studies of individuals (with identifying features altered) whose stories I have known intimately through my 30-plus years of practice and who aptly represent the tremendous challenges of burnout and the very real possibilities of self-care. Finally, there are questions at the conclusion of most chapters, designed for personal examination and understanding. It may be that these opportunities for reflection will also have value to those important to you, either in social work and related professions or not. Hopefully, new areas of self-awareness can lead to clearer individualized direction as well as more meaningful and fulfilling sharing and communication with others. Authentic, trusting contact is a gift synonymous with self-care.

In social work and related mental health professions, although we are surrounded by people all day long, there is not a balanced give and take. The concentration is on clients, not ourselves. In the truest sense, we are alone: We are the givers, and our professional fulfillment comes from seeing the growth, hope, and new direction in those with whom we are privileged to work. The fulfillment of our professional commitment demands that we do our best and give as much as possible in the ethical ways that are the underpinnings of our social work profession. With this awareness, common sense predicts that burnout is a potential threat waiting for us in the wings. However, as we all know, common sense and clear thinking can be eroded when our own "unfinished emotional business" (Scarf, 1995) propels us.

My life and work have taught me that the strongest lesson in avoiding burnout through self-care is to accept that we are human, and in that, we are each limited and, yes, flawed. Despite best intentions and very hard work, we will each experience failure, and our losses and the losses of those dear to us will bring the most unbearable pain imaginable.

Yet, with all of the pain and loss of life, we can, if we will it, grow, learn, and move forward in our life journey. If we hold on to this, we can understand how important self-care is. It will give us the strength to claim the joys of living and endure what we must. And it will help us to ensure that our clients are able, whenever possible, to do the same.

PART 1
Burnout

Burnout

Chapter 1

What Is Burnout?

I was startled when I read the following words from one of our questionnaire respondents (hereinafter, respondents): "I feel like there should be a healthy fear of entering the social work field" (Respondent #60). To me, these words underscore the necessity of preparing for what we will find in our chosen field. I would not choose the word "fear," but I am convinced that all of us as social workers, from the time we are students, must have a healthy awareness of what the choice of a social work profession means, how it will affect us, and how to prepare for these realities.

If you have chosen social work, you most likely already know that it is not a field synonymous with prestige or recognition. Social workers do not ever expect a producer from *any* of the network morning news shows to call explaining that they are planning a show focusing on our commitment to bringing hope and confidence to the most vulnerable among our population. Further, in most traditional social work settings, we are not going to be as well paid as many of those who have chosen to pursue different degrees. When we share the kinds of work we do in conversation with others, we usually do not receive the excited and respectful responses reserved for professions seen as more prestigious and exciting. A fellow colleague puts it this way: "Our work just isn't seen as sexy!" This means that we must experience and feel the excitement and opportunity of social work within ourselves.

Even though the body of social work knowledge is prodigious and the impact of social work is enormous, there remains great debate among social workers as to our identity and direction. Outside of our profession, most people do not understand either the work that we do or our profound and constant commitment to creating a society that embodies justice and opportunity. All that we stand for and work toward is largely invisible to others, as well as misunderstood. There are many people who think of us as "touchy feely do-gooders," even if they have the good manners to keep these feelings to themselves. With this as the backdrop to the large responsibilities we carry, it is understandable that social work is a profession in which the incidence of burnout is high, and its ever-present possibility is a specter that looms over all of our professional lives.

Certainly, the possibility of burnout can and does occur in professions other than ours. Just a few months ago, a very good friend who had planned an evening at the theater with my family months before did not arrive at our scheduled destination. When we finally got in touch with her, we learned that our plans completely slipped her mind due to her "exhaustion and depletion" after spending the day with her father at his care facility. It is my hope that readers not in the mental health field will find in these pages approaches to prevent and alleviate burnout that can be helpful, relevant, and meaningful.

Despite the fact that burnout occurs in myriad professions, and can often be seen in the personal lives of those whose work occurs within the home, it was first identified in the mental health professions due to the complex relationship between caregiver and client. (Oser, Biebel, Pullen, & Harp, 2013). One of the motivations for this book is a deep concern about the high drop-out rate of social work professionals who have been trained to work with our most vulnerable population. With this in mind, the primary concentration in this book will be on burnout in the social work profession, with clear parallels to all mental health and related professions. Freudenberger (1974) chose the word "burnout" in part because of its definition in *Merriam-Webster's Dictionary*: "to fail, to wear out, or become exhausted by making excessive demands on energy, strength, or resources" (p. 159). According to Freudenberger, when we are burned out we become increasingly "inoperative." Maslach (1993) further defined burnout as having three chief components: (1) emotional exhaustion (inability to feel compassion for clients), (2) depersonalization (detachment from the emotional needs of their client, and (3) lack of a feeling of personal accomplishment (critical evaluation of oneself). In other words, burnout is a completely understandable human response to emotional and physical overload. To repeat, everyone is susceptible to its onset, but the demands of the mental health field, and social work in particular, make one even more susceptible.

These are the common side effects of what Norcross (2000) called our "grueling and demanding" therapeutic work. Symptoms such as "moderate depression, mild anxiety, emotional exhaustion and disrupted relationships" (p. 710) can be brought on by "inadequate supervision and mentorship, glamorized expectations . . . and acute performance anxiety" (Skovholt, Grier, & Hanson, 2001, p. 170). There is evidence that compassion fatigue increases when a social worker sees that a client's situation is not improving (Corcoran, 1987). Mental health practitioners from all sectors can become inflexible and closed and, as burnout progresses, experience long bouts of irritability and hopelessness in which they resign to feeling ineffective. More serious cases can lead to paranoia, self-medication with legal or illegal substances, or even the end of a promising career. To complicate matters, the nonreciprocal nature of the practitioner–client relationship may lead practitioners to neglect their own needs until suddenly everything seems overwhelming (Skovholt et al., 2001). In short, if we do not recognize the onset of burnout or treat its development with due respect for its potential severity, the consequences may be catastrophic.

In the 40 years since Freudenberger (1974) coined the term, qualitative and quantitative research on burnout has expanded dramatically. Yet, as we examine this research more closely in the coming sections, we will find that clarifications are needed and that questions and challenges regarding burnout remain. Many of Freudenberger's questions remain either unanswered or answered only provisionally, including: What are the early danger signs of burnout? Can it be avoided? Are certain types of people more prone to suffer burnout than others? Are we willing to realize its potential dangers to our clients, our loved ones, and ourselves?

As burnout has become more frequently discussed in the literature, its complexity and dangers have been addressed in our classrooms and professional settings, although rarely to the degree that is truly warranted. Many newly minted social workers lack both the knowledge of what may be transpiring in their lives when symptoms of burnout appear as well as the critical faculties to assess their experience objectively and are therefore unable to take the proper measures to reclaim their equilibrium. Even though undergraduate and graduate school course concentration on burnout has recently begun to be offered, most social workers remain unprepared for the rigors of the profession during their early years of practice.

Burnout is a complex phenomenon that draws its strength from multiple sources. We may be living in a place and time that carries its own personal stresses and dangers, or we may be simply stuck in a rut of perfectionism and "people pleasing" that leaves no room for ourselves and our personal relationships. We may also be experiencing emotional abuse at work. In addition to these considerations, all of us will have issues from our childhood that our clients will echo. When they bring issues to us that we have not faced in ourselves, resistance to burnout and the depression that may well accompany it is greatly impaired. Unless what is touched in us is confronted, understood, and addressed, the components of burnout that Maslach warns of—emotional exhaustion, depersonalization, and a decreased sense of personal accomplishments—will very likely invade our lives. An indication that this invasion has either occurred or is not far away is a social worker's expression of feeling "heart sick" or "soul sick" about what is being experienced and faced.

Some of the previous descriptions will sound like depression to you, for there is overlap in the symptoms of burnout and depression, and the two can be experienced in combination. However, there is also a fairly clear distinction between what causes each. Burnout is a condition brought on by overload, by not seeing a way out, and by the impact of other lives and circumstances with which one is in close contact. Depression, on the other hand, is usually associated with life events, such as death of a loved one, onset of illness in one's family or in the family of one dear to you, divorce, or betrayal; or its origin may be undetermined, with no understanding of what has caused it. Stress and anxiety can be associated with both burnout and depression as we attempt to adapt to burdensome experiences. Negativity accompanies both.

One poignant example of the combination of burnout and depression involves a husband or wife tirelessly caring for a cherished partner or parent. Again and again, in these instances, I have heard exhausted, overwhelmed caretakers speak of mourning the loss of the vibrant person they knew, shared with, and loved. Another example of the combination involves caring for a child who is severely ill and will not recover. In these tragic life events, again and again, parents entering therapy tell me that their hopes and dreams have been destroyed, replaced only by anguish.

Although it is my strong hope that the self-care strategies in this book can be effective in easing the sorrow and suffering involved in both burnout and depression, the focus and discussion will revolve around the concept of burnout encountered by social workers and mental health professionals due to the nature of their work, their work environments, and their lack of preparedness and proactive approaches.

Because burnout has proven to be such a complex phenomenon, researchers have found it useful to explore burnout through various related aspects or what might be called attendant syndromes, including compassion fatigue (Figley, 2005); countertransference (Pearlman & Saakvitne, 1995); and vicarious traumatization (Pearlman & Mac Ian, 1995), which, for the sake of ease, has been shortened to vicarious trauma in much of the literature and in other places is referred to as secondary traumatic stress (Figley, 1995; Stamm, 1995). Although there is some overlap among the three attendant syndromes of burnout, each of them presents a particular lens through which it is valuable to view the experience of burnout.

It should be noted, however, that while countertransference and vicarious trauma are very real aspects of burnout, each has a more specific purview.

Compassion fatigue, on the other hand, can exist alone. However, it is always a component of the other two expressions of burnout. Further, what will become clear as we move on in our examination of burnout is that social workers and others in related fields are prone to burnout, not only because of the nature of our work but often also because of our own natures. With this in mind, it is important to understand that the challenges each of us face in balancing our life–work interaction will be more easily addressed through knowledge that addresses why burnout occurs. For the remaining part of this chapter, I will concentrate on each attendant syndrome individually, bearing in mind the connections and potential overlap between them. I will also present illustrative case studies of individuals with whom I have been acquainted in over 30 years in the field, and conclude, as I will in future chapters, with opportunities for reflection.

Compassion Fatigue

Compassion fatigue is the broadest of the three perspectives through which to view burnout in our professional lives. It describes the emotional and physical fatigue that social workers and those in related professions may experience due to "the chronic use of empathy when treating patients who are suffering in some way" (Newell & MacNeil, 2010, p. 61). Helping or wanting to help a traumatized or suffering person can result in compassion fatigue (Figley, 1995), especially when we do not receive relief from the burden and the responsibility that such exposure places on us (Fox, 2003).

You may notice in this chapter that compassion and empathy are used somewhat interchangeably; in chapter 3, when transforming compassion fatigue into "compassion satisfaction" is discussed, it will become clear that the road to compassion satisfaction is accomplished by appreciating the value of empathy over the related concepts of sympathy or pity. Chapter 3 will also note that there are differences between empathy and compassion, each necessary for the recovery of our clients and for our own protection against burnout. A lack of empathy for clients poses a profound danger to their treatment and can result in the their retraumatization (Dane, 2002). Further, without empathy, our own road from compassion fatigue to compassion satisfaction cannot be realized and protected.

One of our respondents described the condition of compassion fatigue in some of his colleagues as like "an old car that wasn't maintained; they're thin in the metal and not running as well as they used to be." He continued, "They give their all in service to others and now they've become worn out, through a combination of long-term service and exposure. . . . They stay in their careers and continue to provide good helpful service, but they're tired and need help with self-care" (Respondent #34). This respondent thought "rust-out" would be a better term than "burnout" for those who fall into this category. One individual with whom I became well acquainted exhibited this rusted-out quality of burnout, which for many social workers is the first evidence that burnout exists:

Michelle worked as a social worker in family court where I first met her. I was there as an expert witness to give testimony in a case over a period of several days, during which time Michelle and I became well acquainted. Over lunch in the courthouse cafeteria, she confided that when she came home from work at night, regardless of how she tried, she could not escape the voices in her head of those she had given her all to during the day. "I just cannot control or shut these voices off. The screaming adults and the tears of those hurting and frightened, especially the children, are the most unbearable," she told me. Though her sister, whom Michelle lived with, wanted to go out with her during the week on occasion, and always on the weekends, Michelle felt too exhausted for the companionship with her sister that she had so enjoyed in previous years. In addition, she lost interest in any general socializing or meeting new people. She described the constant upheavals in her clients' lives as "a totally exhausting emotional assault on my senses that feels almost physical." Instead of being sociable, in order to calm herself, Michelle turned to several glasses of wine and mindless TV each night. In fact, once finally home, her cat was the only living being she could bear to feel close to. When Michelle was finally able to sleep, she (and her sister) were awakened with regularity by Michelle's nightmares relating to the travails of the families with whom she worked. This constant turmoil is not what Michelle was seeking or expecting when she chose social work as her profession. She wanted to help bring what she describes as "light and hope" into her clients' lives. Instead, however, as time passed and she could not leave her responsibilities at work, she increasingly found herself keeping her clients at arm's length, unwilling or unable to engage with her new assignees fully. Her sense of depletion heightened, turning into a callousness, verging on bitterness, that shocked her.

Many types of work can become grinds, but social workers experience a very specific form of hopelessness brought on by compassion fatigue. Such hopelessness might manifest itself, as it did in Michelle's case, by a social worker saying to himself or herself, "I cannot wait to go home and numb myself with alcohol." Some of the other common expressions of compassion fatigue referenced by our respondents included the following:

"I should have chosen a different profession."
"Why am I still here?"
"What is my purpose?"

"Why bother?"

"What difference are we really making?"

"What is the point if no one cares?"

"I am not contributing in a meaningful way."

"I don't even want to go to work."

"I cannot make it through this day."

Compassion fatigue is real, but we can only work on alleviating this aspect of burnout if we take ourselves and our own needs seriously. In all mental health professions, though we are surrounded by our clients and coworkers, the intent of our actions is to improve the well-being of others, not ourselves. If we do our work well, the concentration will always be on our clients, and in this sense, then, we are alone. There is no balanced give and take; instead we may feel like Coleridge's Ancient Mariner, who, adrift on a windless ocean, suffers from a terrible thirst along with the rest of his shipmates. The Mariner complains that although he sees "Water, water everywhere" there is not a single "drop to drink" (Coleridge, 1965).

We are the givers, and our fulfillment comes from seeing the growth, hope and new direction in those with whom we are privileged to work. The fulfillment of our professional commitment demands that we do our best and give as much as possible within the ethical guidelines of our profession. With this awareness, common sense would dictate that burnout is a potential reality: that, far too often, even when we leave our social work clients and settings, we will inevitably take visions and voices of our clients home with us. This inability to have a clear distinction between our work and our life makes us unable to return to our personal worlds and find the necessary relaxation, enjoyment, and fulfillment to sustain and energize us. Common sense and clear thinking can then be easily and predictably eroded.

Countertransference

Although there are many in the helping professions who describe fulfilling childhoods that are secure and stable, research indicates that the majority who come into our field have known profound pain and loss during their formative years (Elliott & Guy, 1993). Elliott and Guy (1993) found, for example, that women working in the mental health professions were more frequently traumatized as children by physical abuse, alcoholism, emotional and sexual abuse, and familial conflict than were women working in other fields. In addition, therapists appeared to come from more chaotic families of origin, with significantly fewer experiences of familial cohesion, moral emphasis, and achievement orientation. In a study comparing psychotherapists and physicists, psychotherapists were significantly more likely to perceive themselves as assuming a care-taking role than were physicists (Fussell & Bonney, 1990). The same study showed that psychotherapists also experienced significantly more parent–child role inversion (*parentification*) than did the physicists: It is understandable that a codependent parenting role can easily spill over into boundary violations with clients. Commonly, those in social work and other mental health professions have experienced one or a combination of five patterns of emotional abuse: rage, enmeshment, rejection/abandonment, severe neglect, and overprotection and overindulgence (Smullens, 2010). Rage, enmeshment, rejection/abandonment, and neglect can lead to a strong desire to give to others what we know is longed for, coupled by an inability to care for oneself to counteract exhaustion.

Thus, not only does a social worker's daily milieu provide the occasion for experiencing burnout, but many social workers are themselves inherently more vulnerable to its impact via the aspect of burnout known as *countertransference*. Countertransference was originally defined by Freud (1912 /1958) as the result of the patient's influence on the practitioner's unconscious feelings and later expanded by Winnicott (1949) and Kernberg (1965) to include the broader experience of a therapist's conscious and appropriate total reaction to his or her client. Countertransference then occurs naturally and becomes a problem only when we take on the psychological realities of our clients with no clear sense of boundaries between our experience and theirs. It may be built directly into the very fabric of the kind of work we do. As Fox (2003) put it, "Ironically, our empathic ability makes us particularly susceptible to emotional contagion, experiencing the feelings of the sufferer" (p. 48).

With this in mind, it becomes imperative to be continually aware that we strive for a relationship with our clients that is based on mutual respect, one that is collaborative yet still retains essential boundaries. Achieving this balance and differentiation necessitates concern for our clients but also an appropriate degree of distance or detachment, where the client is always seen as an individual separate from us, and our objectivity is protected for the good of the therapeutic relationship and the growth of each client.

Our goal with a client is never one that is reciprocal. Violating the boundaries of a therapeutic alliance does far more than jeopardize the client–social worker relationship. Mistaking a successful therapeutic bond with a client for something more than a professional relationship can lead to both destruction of an ongoing therapeutic relationship and grave injury to the client. Further, slipping beyond appropriate recognition of our role can lead to unethical actions, such as entering into a close personal friendship with a client or developing a sexual relationship. Examples of more subtle boundary challenges include how missed appointments are to be handled (though each social work setting has a great deal to say about this), maintaining an appropriate financial relationship with our clients, and how we conduct ourselves when we unexpectedly meet a client in our day-to-day lives outside of our offices

Countertransference, however, may reflect a deeper inability to say no, which increases the likelihood of succumbing to inappropriate professional relationships and is one of the hazards of the profession that can complicate work that is already difficult (Skovholt et al., 2001). A social worker may be burned out, lonely, facing an aching emptiness within, yet be totally unaware of this debilitating state. Never realizing it, he or she may be turning to the profession as a way to escape this inner turmoil. In other words, by picking a so-called helping profession, one may be asking for one's own personal help.

If this is true of you, do not let it frighten you. This is true of many who select social work and related professions. Further, it is a healthy and effective coping strategy that children who face trauma in their homes (almost always with no words to give to their pain) learn in order to protect themselves. In other words, dealing with one's own fears by being drawn to help others is a highly effective defense mechanism. If this is true for you, facing it is a very brave, positive, and helpful first step. As we will see, those who face this reality about themselves, as well as other truths involving their formative experiences and the impact of these experiences, also create capacities for fulfilling, meaningful lives, personally and professionally.

The reality of countertransference means that, as social workers, we will become extremely exhausted if we are not in constant touch with factors that clients bring to us that touch our core. This means that we must constantly think about both the client and ourselves. The paradox, of course, is that we may have chosen social work specifically because all we want to do (in order not to face past pain and perhaps present difficulties in our own lives) is to help others, which we are now doing unknowingly at the expense of our own well-being.

Again and again, our discussion underscores the importance of keeping in mind that quality work cannot be offered without clear boundaries that are critical to the healing process. When the trauma presented by our clients touches unresolved conflicts of our own, a combination of skilled supervision and increased introspection to understand ourselves can help to ensure the continuity of the necessary safe holding environment that our clients require (Dane, 2002). Dombo and Gray pointed out that understanding countertransference can help us make "a clear distinction between 'taking in' what the client is experiencing, and 'taking on' the client's experience" (2013, p. 92). This is the difference between leaving our work at the office and taking it home and acting it out in our own lives inappropriately, to our own detriment.

Because "unfinished emotional business" (Scarf, 1995) can and does affect all aspects of our personal and professional lives, social workers can protect ourselves by reflecting on what is being touched in us by our clients and by asking ourselves: Do we have issues with members of our family of origin that are unresolved and drain present relationships, keeping us from seeing clearly? Do we long to establish closeness with a family member who has continuously made it clear that this is not a mutual desire? Without realizing it, are we hoping that friends and acquaintances will take the place of loved ones who, for various reasons, are no longer in our lives? Are there present issues regarding a partner or sexual preference? Are we struggling to find the intimacy we crave yet which still eludes us? The list, in myriad forms, can go on and on. It is essential to remember that when our clients bring these very same issues to us that we have not faced, burnout and the depression that can accompany it can set in, leading to emotional exhaustion, depersonalization, and a decreased sense of personal accomplishments.

Vicarious Trauma

Vicarious trauma results from a social worker's direct exposure to victims of trauma. This aspect of burnout refers to the emotions that result from knowing about a traumatizing event experienced by a client and the stress resulting from helping or wanting to help this person (Bell, Kulkarni, & Dalton, 2003). The symptoms can be the same as those of post-traumatic stress disorder, for which it was named: persistent reexperiencing of symptoms from the past; avoiding places, events, or objects that are reminders of an experience; or being easily startled and feeling tense or on edge (American Psychiatric Association, 2013).

As noted earlier, each of these three categories—compassion fatigue, countertransference, and vicarious trauma—are aspects of burnout, and rigid separations between them in theory does not echo the real-life experiences of those in our field. Trauma can be experienced in a way very similar to the aforementioned description of countertransference. In fact, the term *traumatic countertransference* has been used to describe a social worker's emotional feelings for a trauma survivor and the traumatic events that are being discussed (Dane, 2002).

Nonetheless, vicarious trauma identifies a very specific face of burnout, namely, "the effects which graphic and painful material (for example, death, violence, injury, 9/11) presented to us by different individuals produces in our own cognitive schemas or belief, expectations, and assumptions about ourselves and others" (Fox, 2003, p. 48). Sometimes referred to as *secondary traumatiza-tion* or *secondary traumatic stress,* this experience impedes our ability to attend appropriately to another's experience and issues (Fox, 2003).

According to Humphrey (2013), hearing the traumatic stories of others can affect our own worldview and sense of security. This places practitioners who are not prepared to manage their feelings associated with hearing traumatic stories of others at risk of burnout. One of our respondents described an experience of vicarious trauma this way:

> I suffered the most intensely when I worked in the 9/11 program at the time of the anniversaries. Our staff volunteered each year at the site and in the family room (a makeshift memorial . . . [area for] family members that overlooked the site). These were taxing times. I felt dread, fatigue, tear-fulness, irritability, helplessness, physical aches, and moments of [being] overwhelm[ed]. (Respondent #14)

In the preceding case involving 9/11, the extraordinary pain and suffering of grieving families after a national crisis will understandably cause a social worker to struggle to maintain energy and concentration while navigating appropriate boundaries. Yet, this trauma is compounded when the personal is also professional, such as when a social worker himself or herself has been exposed to the same traumatic occurrence, as in the events of 9/11 (Tosone, Nuttman-Shwartz, & Stephens, 2012). In these cases of "shared trauma," an extra layer of difficulty is encountered.

Another challenging aspect of social work may be surviving vicarious trauma when exposed to those who commit monstrous acts, such as rape, murder, torture, and other forms of violation of others. What social workers see is often unbelievable to most. As one respondent said, "You just can't make this stuff up" (Respondent #17).

Of course, the monstrous acts all have heard about and even witnessed in newscasts that show those without capacity for compassion toward the suffering of others—those who seem to have ice water in their veins and those who can find release and pleasure tormenting, terrorizing, and killing—have made the general public more aware of inhumanity, brutality, and torture. Still, as shocked, sickened, angry, and overwhelmed as those who see or learn of these murders and atrocities become, most believe abuse and brutal acts are more isolated in our own communities than they actually are.

Social workers, psychiatrists, psychologists, and those in related fields know well that sadistic pathology can exist all around us. We know that appearances can be deceiving and that not all who are dangerous are isolated from friends, families, and neighbors. We know also that cruelty can be found in homes of all cultures and socioeconomic backgrounds; that although we may have hints and clues, no one can truly know the lives of others behind closed doors; and that the same person capable of brutality of innocents can be described by others as mild mannered, kind, funny, generous, and can even be a community leader.

Clinicians in most mental health professions address internal problems, relationship conflicts, and self-defeating attitudes and behaviors. Yet, unlike social workers and those who share related employment, most are not confronted with the underbelly of the real world in their day-to-day work. We, however, day in and day out, come face-to-face with abuse of every kind, often in the very settings in which they occur—abuse compounded by poverty, hopelessness, and hunger.

Part of a social worker's belief is that everyone can change; but, that said, we also know there are those who have no desire to change. We walk into houses and see couches that are so infested with fleas and bedbugs that we dare not sit down, for if we do, we will be eaten up from head to toe. We have seen rats the size of kittens. We work with parents and caretakers who have abused their children emotionally, physically, and sexually. We have seen food money used for drugs. We have seen children who have never been taken to a doctor or dentist. We have seen children who have been starved and tortured, whose genitalia have been burned for masturbating, and whose entire little bodies have been used as human ashtrays. Indeed, what we see you cannot make up.

What we see firsthand and the impact of our vicarious trauma can be very difficult, if not impossible, to communicate to non–social workers and those not in related mental health professions. A similar dynamic exists when those on the battlefields of war return home. Most just want to do all they can to forget what they have witnessed, been part of, and endured. Most never even try to discuss this with anyone, for in the words of one of my clients regarding his three tours of duty in Vietnam, "Who will want to hear about it? Who could believe what I have seen? I cannot ever speak about what I have done." The father of a friend, who had served in World War II, fell into a deep depression after *The Greatest Generation*, by Tom Brokaw, was published in 1998. Brokaw's book, which gave enormous praise to the courage and grit of those who carried the Allies to victory, was issued to rave reviews. My friend's father, however, was deeply unsettled and angered by its publication. Though he refused to read it, the praise heaped on him drove him to despair: "They do not understand what really happened. To the readers, the war was a contest we won, like something they have seen on TV. I am praised undeservedly! I did not want to remember what was necessary, what it took, to win," he told his son. "I did not ever want to allow my thoughts to go back to these times." He continued, "When people began telling me what a hero I was, their compliments made me remember all I had pushed out of my mind: the death of fellow soldiers, the killing of other human beings, endless terror and suffering. I began to feel sick and slip once again into what I have tried to escape my whole life, the bloody hell of war."

Predictably in your own family of loved and trusted ones, as well as with your own well-meaning, educated friends, you will find that many do not understand what your work brings you, day in and day out. If you try to tell them, they may well respond with rationalization and denial. For the truths of your work may be too painful and upsetting for them to even hear about.

What Is Burnout? A Case Study

This combination of the inability to share your work with friends and loved ones and your own lack of understanding of what the inhumane violations you see touch in you can lead to feelings of isolation and exhaustion. The following is an example from work with Connie, a second-year MSW student, who was placed in a prison setting for her field work:

In her first year of graduate school, Connie had excelled in both her academic work and her work with clients. However, as skilled as she was, certain cases in her second year of training caused her to feel ill and repulsed. During this period, Connie developed an ongoing skin condition that she had not had before graduate school. For reasons her doctors could not determine, large pustules began to erupt all over her arms.

Connie considered dropping out of graduate school. An English major in college, she was offered a job in a highly regarded public relations firm. It was an unsolicited offer, made by one of her former English professors who now worked in the firm. The job was described as "draining and pressured, but fun and lucrative." Only the first half of this description seemed to apply to what awaited her as a social worker! Still, Connie decided to persist with her MSW degree and a placement that she knew would continue to ask a great deal of her.

During her field placement in prison, Connie was assigned a client who was accused not only of embezzlement, but also of killing his wife so that he could marry his mistress. James faced the death penalty. Connie was expected to work with him throughout her second year and then to return to the prison following graduation (as partial payment toward the scholarship and living stipend she had received from the center that employed her).

James had become very close to a priest who visited the prison weekly, and through this trusted relationship, Connie was assigned as James' social worker. There was always a guard with Connie during her time with James, but he was a kind and discreet one, who liked James and was as unobtrusive as possible during their biweekly meetings. In their work together, Connie learned that James had been abandoned by his father when his mother was pregnant with him. She also learned that James' mother was a drug-addicted prostitute who at times tried to be clean but could not maintain sobriety of any sort. Her pimp was a ruthless monster, but the only available father figure during James's formative years. In James's words:

> I learned everything awful from him, including how to treat women, but at least he was there. No one else was. He often made me scrambled eggs for breakfast. No one else ever did that, and on the days I went to school, he was the one who took me. Then after school, he and I would have catches. This was the only fun I ever knew as a kid.

Not all inmates on death row become introspective. Obviously, some become more hardened, furious, and bitter, taking no responsibility for their actions. Some claim their innocence throughout their internment. And as we know from the latest DNA investigations and new, refined research, some are truly innocent, and their arrest, internment, and death are a travesty. But none of these examples was the case with James. He knew all he had done was vile, and he was deeply sorry. He had no doubt that the kindness and love shown him by the priest made this self-reflection, assessment, and attempts at repentance possible. In his words, "Father John was the first man in my life to be kind and decent in every aspect of his dealings with others." And James added: "Plus Father brought Connie into my world, and she has been a blessing."

With Connie as his social worker, James was able to recount all of his ruthless horror; and Connie learned, through superb supervision, to listen, to care, and to show the compassion that only she and Father John had ever given to James. She learned the importance of a coping strategy her professors and supervisor referred to as "compassionate judgment." In her words, "What James did was awful, horrific, but during his most important formative years, 'awful and horrific' is all he knew."

There were many appeals to save James's life, and Father John and Connie always wrote and testified on his behalf, but James would not be spared. In the second year of Connie's employment at the prison, James died in the electric chair. Father John and Connie were allowed to be with him for an hour before his walk to the death chamber. They promised to be looking right at him through the glass as he took his final breath. And they were.

Through this work with James, Connie learned to understand that in her future as a social worker she would not be able to erase the horrors many of her clients faced as children or the full impact of these horrors. What she could do, however, was provide a healing presence to her clients: She could be there with them, believe in them, and advocate for them. Further, though her strong social work relationship with James, Connie forged a new definition of forgiveness that extended well beyond her work with clients. In her words, "I learned the essential difference between 'to condone' and 'to forgive,' and that one way to forgive is to work hard to understand why people do what they do, as well as how they developed to be the human beings they have become."

Safeguarding Professional Standards

One thing is clear: Through the agencies of compassion fatigue, countertransference, and vicarious trauma, burnout can systematically decrease not only our ability to find meaning, direction, and fulfillment in our own lives, but also our ability to relate successfully to our clients and coworkers. Each of these draining manifestations can make it impossible to maintain the essential distinction between practitioner and client and in this way do our jobs well, thus striking at the heart of our self-identification as one who cared about healing and contributing to the health of our community.

Compounding this frustration, despite our best attempts, community resources, rather than improve, may remain the same, or even worsen, further increasing our disaffection for our work and leading to disconnection and isolation, both professional and personally.

Other things are clear also: Stress is part and parcel of our professional lives, and awareness and self-care can help us to manage it. Most of our clients will heal slowly; and predictably, after taking two steps forward, they will take one or more steps backward. We must recognize this as part of the process of growth and change.

Compassion fatigue, countertransference, and vicarious trauma are three experiences that every social worker and those in related fields will experience again and again and again in our professional lives. We can reduce our stress and frustration by understanding these internal reactions, by learning to recognize them, and by understanding how they overlap and influence each other. As an example, vicarious trauma can increase and provoke compassion fatigue, while the origins of compassion fatigue may also be found in an individual social worker's psychosocial history, which, though acted out with a client, is not seen or understood because of blinding countertransference.

In this way, as will become clearer in coming chapters, we learn how to separate ourselves from our clients, knowing that despite how deeply we care, our clients' journeys are theirs, not ours, and that there will always be realities in their lives and in our communities over which we have no control.

Questions for Reflection

At this juncture, you may be thinking about your own responses to the questions that this chapter poses. Below are several questions for reflection you may want to consider as you assess your own current relative state of burnout; each chapter that follows will contain similar questions for your reflection.

- Do you self-medicate with drugs or alcohol? Do you find that your intake of such substances increases on more stressful days, when you experience an intense schedule or a particular session that hits too closely to home?
- What is the impact on you when sessions leave you unsettled because they did not go as you had hoped?
- How do you deal with sessions in which you recognize that you have missed some important client signals?
- Even if exhausted, when you leave work, do you feel satisfied that you have worked hard and to the best of your ability? Or do you feel dizzy with exhaustion, nearly unable to function or incapable of functioning in your personal world?
- Do you watch other people in their jobs and assume they are happier or more fulfilled than you are?
- Do you have intrusive thoughts during a session, wishing you were somewhere else, doing something else?
- Do you have angry outbursts at home or with the people whom you love and who love you, seemingly for no reason?
- Do you daydream about being able to retire from your profession or move on to doing something different with your life at a time in the future, perhaps the very near future?
- Are you often late for work? Do you take the opportunity to call in sick when nothing is seriously wrong?
- Have you experienced a large fluctuation in your weight recently (either gain or loss)?

- Do you feel that no one really understands what you go through at work? Do you long for someone to be able to understand what you cope with day in and day out?
- Do you have trouble falling asleep or sleeping through the night? Do you need medication to help you sleep?
- Are there those important to you, either in the mental health field or not, who are experiencing some of the symptoms and reactions noted? If so, perhaps the following pages will also have relevance for them.

Chapter 2
Arenas of Burnout

In chapter 1, we looked at three different overlapping categories of burnout that affect each of us: compassion fatigue, countertransference, and vicarious trauma. In this chapter, we will resume our discussion by looking at burnout in a broader context: the demographic and vocational variables that affect burnout and the four arenas in which burnout can make its most powerful impact. These four arenas are the professional (that is, one's place of employment), the personal (including the psychological, emotional, cognitive, intellectual, and spiritual/religious experiences of the practitioner), the social (including an individual's relationships with partners, family, friends, and community), and the physical (pertaining to the practitioner's body). Looking at these four arenas closely is especially crucial as they prefigure the location, style, and context of the various types of self-care that can be used to alleviate certain manifestations of burnout.

It is important to note at the outset that these distinctions are for the sake of clarity of discussion. In reality, burnout is a complex phenomenon, one that develops in and affects multiple facets of our lives. Just as countertransference cannot be separated cleanly from compassion fatigue or vicarious trauma, so burnout at work can be complicated by many factors in a social worker's life, such as a lack of support at home (Radey & Figley, 2007). It stands to reason that the depleted psychological state of a social worker suffering from burnout can lead to moderate to severe physical issues, which will then further compound an impaired sense of well-being. Therefore, as we begin to make sense of burnout, it is essential that we bear in mind not only its complex components but also its systemic interactive nature.

Variables Affecting Burnout

One recent review of the literature posited five factors that may be related to burnout: age, gender, professional seniority, family status, and education level (Hamama, 2012). Regarding age in particular, four of the studies reviewed showed that burnout was more prevalent in social workers under the age of 30. Researchers suggested that older individuals were more emotionally, financially, and socially stable than those just starting out. Social work students may view this as a cause for concern; however, the opposite perspective can also be taken: One can derive comfort from studies that indicate burnout decreases with age. As we get older, we are better able to handle stress; our perspectives have matured, and we have developed the ability to select and maintain more fulfilling relationships that can be relied on for mutual sharing and support.

Hamama's (2012) recent review of the literature related to burnout reported these additional observations:

- Gender. Research showed that burnout was more prevalent among female social workers than among males, perhaps attributable to the number of women in emotionally demanding human service professions.
- Professional seniority. Those individuals in higher positions of authority or seniority were generally exposed to more challenging roles and rewards than those with low seniority and thus were less vulnerable to burnout.
- Family status. Single female social workers reported higher rates of burnout than married social workers, a finding that was linked to married women (no data were analyzed regarding men) having a greater emotional and financial support system.
- Level of education. Interestingly, the higher the level of education, the more likely the incidence of burnout. Researchers attributed this correlation to the frustration that some more highly educated social workers felt at being overqualified for certain positions or being unable to advance in their organizations.

It is important to note that none of these studies was normative; that is, they were not definitive in isolating a single demographic that was destined for burnout. The above studies are noted only because they illuminate some of the ingredients of burnout, such as a lack of an emotional support system or obstacles to professional advancement.

A recent study of social workers in the fields of child protection and welfare that may have a greater degree of correlation with longevity in the social work profession, and thus by implication with a lower rate of burnout, or at least a greater ability to manage burnout, was done in 2011 by Kenneth Burns. In brief, the researcher separated social workers into three categories based on their intent of joining the social work profession: those choosing the profession consciously out of school as a "career preference"; those who regarded social work as a stepping stone to other career paths, the "transients"; and those who joined the profession later in life, the "converts". Burns (2011) found that the "transients"—who were the least convinced that they would remain in the profession and were the most skeptical about their career choice—had the highest incidence of burnout. The lowest levels of burnout were reported by the "converts," who had come to social work with more life experience and a greater degree of self-knowledge. Burns reported, "While all of the social workers in the study 'chose' to enter child protection and welfare, there are different motivations for doing so, which, in turn, influence the length of social workers' tenure expectations and the likelihood of their retention" (p. 534).

All of the variables mentioned earlier need to be acknowledged for the light that they can shed on the origins of burnout. With that said, mastering the self-care strategies presented in the second half of this book is a far greater predictor of surviving burnout than belonging to any demographic condition or category of professional intent. The previously mentioned studies are presented to help readers ascertain where their particular stressors are located. Sometimes these causes are straightforward, such as a particular caseload, both in terms of the number of cases and the countertransference occasioned by the cases. The causes may also be a supervisor's inability to provide a certain needed quality of assistance. Or a cause may be elemental, such as facing a cold, gray season of the year: One of our respondents reported feeling more burned out in the winter, a simple yet powerful cause that she was able to counteract in part by proactive strategies, such as purchasing a UV lamp for her desk and taking long walks whenever she could find sun to warm her. (Respondent #8).

Areas of Burnout

Throughout the literature devoted to burnout and self-care, there are several different strategies for categorizing the types of self-care that can counteract the effects of burnout. One such designation divides self-care into those practices that affect one's spiritual, mental, emotional, social, and physical well-being (Moore, Bledsoe, Perry, & Robinson, 2011). Another introduces seven categories, divided into five larger groups: spiritual, emotional and psychological, social, physical, and leisure and professional (Lee & Miller, 2013).

However, there has been no attempt, to my knowledge, to connect self-care efforts with the arenas where burnout is directly experienced. Yet, this is precisely what is necessary to protect ourselves from burnout and to counteract its impact. To make this important connection, I will propose the following four-part designation of burnout as it is experienced in four discrete areas of life noted earlier in this chapter: the professional, the personal (or internal), the social, and the physical, as these are the four specific arenas where self-care must be practiced.

Burnout: Professional

At first glance, professional burnout may seem to override and dominate all of the other arenas in which burnout can be experienced; a social worker may see his or her vocation in isolation from other aspects of his or her life. When this is the case, we perceive that our job is what is affecting our internal state, our social relationships, and our physical health.

The reality of burnout, however, is that all four arenas—professional, personal, social, and physical—actually exist in a feedback loop. We may first experience burnout at our job; yet we may also experience a telling personal wake-up call, such as recurring nightmares with similar themes or a desire to numb ourselves with drugs, alcohol, or other addictive behaviors, such as indiscriminant sexual choices. There may be trouble in our intimate relationships and in our close friendships. There may be a breakdown in our physical health to a minor, or even incapacitating, degree.

When we first notice professional burnout, it may ironically be in our struggles to get to work in the first place. Some of our respondents noted the following types of recurring negative ideations when experiencing burnout:

"I don't even want to go to work."
"I cannot make it through this day."
"This is killing me."
"I wish I could just stay home and hide."
"I'm miserable."

Some of these negative ideations were aimed directly at the situation where the social workers found themselves:

"I cannot continue with this schedule."
"I just can't fix everything."
"I am starting to hate the place I work, it feels like I am in a fast-food-type therapy office."

"I'm not good at being a politician."

"I suck at supervising staff—why even try?"

"I really need help with this and there isn't any."

At other times it was aimed at the social worker himself or herself:

"I don't know how to change this."

"I am not paying attention to everything I need to pay attention to."

"My clients are not making progress."

"I am failing my clients."

Within one's professional environment, burnout can occur in reference to one's organization (understanding that sometimes the organization is a stand-in for frustration with society as a whole, laws and lawmakers, or the prevailing attitude of society); one's supervisor; one's coworkers; or one's own professional competence. A combination of these factors can lead to an overwhelming feeling of powerlessness, which was a common theme among respondents: "There are so many families in need, yet so many of the services are full or are so overcrowded that they are no longer even therapeutically beneficial" (Respondent #6). This respondent felt depleted by various forms of bureaucracy: "The government just does not seem to know what social workers really need to be effective. These regulations are more of a hindrance than a help" (Respondent #6).

When we experience burnout in our organizations, the face of that burnout is often our supervisor. This may not be entirely fair, as the supervisor is undoubtedly subject to the same kind of organizational, governmental, and political pressures as the individual social worker and likely at a more intense level. Nonetheless, a common experience is reflected in these words of one respondent: "Rarely does a practitioner feel free to discuss experiences of burnout with a supervisor due to the potential for either direct or indirect termination as a result" (Respondent #16). This honest sharing highlights an obvious catch-22 predicament: When social workers cannot discuss burnout at work, it is much more difficult to remain healthy and effective. However, even in organizations where burnout is discussed at staff meetings, there may not be much empathy offered by supervisors or colleagues. As one respondent put it, "Usually we are told to be happy that we have a job" (Respondent #20).

The following example highlights how essential it is for social workers to understand the strengths and limitations in their settings and to know to whom to turn in highly complex challenges and situations.

Margaret was a psychologist in a mental health setting in a large, highly regarded liberal arts college. One morning, a freshman student came to her office, bruised and hysterical. As she gasped for air, the student explained that in the early morning a male student had come into her room and raped her. On hearing this story, the head of the mental health setting and Margaret's supervisor were in complete agreement. They told her to be wary of these kinds of complaints: "They can give schools a bad reputation, and the question of mutual consent is 'very tricky.'" Hearing these words, Margaret thought to herself: "Mutual consent to an intruder who rapes?"

Neither Margaret's supervisor nor the head of the clinic were unethical or uncaring people, blind to the horrors of rape. However, both needed their jobs, and Margaret knew that their directives came directly from college leadership. She also realized at this point that what was necessary was creative thinking and strategizing, not open confrontation.

Margaret also needed her job, but she also knew that succumbing to fear would be a first step toward depletion and burnout. She knew that if she watched female students suffer and was not able to communicate with leadership about necessary changes, it would be necessary for her to resign.

After giving the serious offense and the college climate careful thought, she decided to act in an effective way by contacting two college professionals whom she trusted, the college attorney, a fearless woman who knew precisely what to do to have the case heard fairly while protecting all concerned, and the college chaplain, a man thoroughly committed to the spiritual growth and confidence of students. Both the attorney and the chaplain had heard of similar cases recently going unaddressed, and this was the proverbial straw that broke the camel's back. The attorney took over the case, adhering to bylaws and directives that led to student, faculty, and administration examination of the case, as well as charges brought in criminal court to the alleged student rapist. The chaplain convened a committee of college professionals, both faculty and administration, to begin to conduct seminars, discussions, and workshops on the nature of rape, respectful communication around sexual choices, societal differences in the use of and propriety of aggression, and societal differences in the treatment of women. The offender was found guilty by both bodies; expelled from college; and sentenced to two years of probation, community service, and anger management classes, sending a clear message to all. Margaret remained in her position and became a trusted confidant of many on campus who knew of her courage; she knew she had made a significant difference.

Personal Burnout

Personal burnout can include psychological challenges with one's moods, sense of purpose, or cognitive distortions created by anxiety or depression. When professional burnout is overlooked or ignored by organization leadership, not addressed by a supervisor, and not discussed or shared between colleagues, the experience is destined to trickle down and rest with the individual social worker. Social workers facing this kind of burden are likely to target themselves. The reasons, at least in part, are that we feel committed to our clients' well-being and see ourselves as the only variable we have the power to change. This trickle-down effect can be seen in some of the recurring negative ideations noted from some respondents:

"I am going to fail this client."
"I am not effective as a clinician."
"How can I help anyone else when I can't even help myself?"

It is human nature to compare our problems to those of our clients, even as thoughts such as these serve to deepen and complicate the cycle of burnout. One may think, "How can I allow myself to feel overwhelmed? I have an education, a job, a roof over my head. I have health insurance. I'm not an incest survivor. I have never been poor or battered. What right have I not to feel wonderful? What's the matter with me? Don't I know how lucky I am?"

It is also important to understand that some of us, because we have seen and known so much suffering, without realizing it, enter our profession to feel needed and important and, in this way, feel better about ourselves. There may be the drive to heal in others what we have been unable to heal in those we love or in ourselves. When this is the case, we insistently tell ourselves, "I can fix this; I can do this; I can carry this." And even, "I must carry this. I must make my effort work for my client!"

This is especially true when a client, despite the highest possible effort of the professional, remains in a state he or she continues to describe as "hopeless," or "a life not worth living," and states in myriad ways, "I cannot find any meaning in my life and anything to live for." As one respondent explained:

> The hardest part was dealing with the suicidality of the clients and worrying about clients who had attempted suicide and expressed suicidal ideation. It was emotionally and spiritually draining and at times made me feel as though I was ineffective and unable to help the clients. (Respondent #60)

As social workers know, this kind of dilemma is one that haunts at the conclusion of a session, for no matter how skilled or seasoned a social worker is, no one can ever be sure of a client's future actions. We must face that there are and will be times, regardless of our efforts, when our work will not motivate change. Further, it can be very hard for one who views himself or herself as being on a continual road to success (and needs to be seen in this way) to recognize and admit the need for help. Compounding a necessary shift and reorientation in accepting professional realities, there is often the growing and unsettling awareness that addressing burnout will not merely involve a cognitive adjustment. As in the following illustration, it may well involve digging more deeply within in order to understand what is being touched in one's self by certain clients, and then what in one's own life has to be addressed and possibly changed or be seen differently, in order to move forward.

Clyde's mother and father were both productive and friendly by all appearances, but, in truth, Clyde's mother had molested her young son with regularity, a fact that he told me for the first time after his mother had passed away. This horror that Clyde was subjected to ended once he began puberty and his mother and father separated; at that time, Clyde's mother began a slow medical decline leading to her death four years later. When Clyde was just 16 years old, he went to live with his maternal grandparents. Although each grandparent was kind to him, Clyde never told either about all he had endured. His reasons were threefold: He feared upsetting two people who cared about him, he did not believe they could ever understand what their daughter had done, and he felt deep shame about his abuse and wanted to do all in his power to push any memories of those years as far as possible from his consciousness.

Despite all he had lived through, rather than become cruel or unkind, Clyde developed into a young man who showed enormous compassion and caring toward others. After high school, he won a state scholarship to college. Upon graduating with honors, he received stipends and loans for his graduate training in social work. Wanting a true family life, the kind he had always longed for, in the early months of his first year in graduate school, Clyde married June, a nursing graduate student close to his age whom he met at their undergraduate university. Their life and love were fulfilling to each until Clyde's second-year field placement with a private agency working with sexually abused young boys and girls.

Immediately after beginning this placement, Clyde began to withdraw not only from sexual intimacy with his wife, but also from every affectionate, loving experience they had shared. No longer did he show interest in the early morning breakfasts they had enjoyed together before their days away from each other began. No longer did he want to plan their weekly movie and supper dates which they fondly had referred to as their "date nights."

At the period in his life when Clyde was referred to me, he felt sure that giving up his career as a social worker was the only way to save his marriage. However, as our work progressed, Clyde slowly began to see things differently.

A naturally introspective young man, Clyde found great relief in understanding and working through the panic he felt in his work setting: "It's like I'm looking into a horrid mirror, and instead of seeing my clients, I see myself. Everything that was done to me in those impossible years passes before my eyes. The only ways I've been able to protect myself from horrible memories are to withdraw and then shut down."

Clyde recognized, of course, that his countertransference was robbing him (and his wife) of all they held dear. Part of his necessary process of healing and, in this way, reclaiming a fulfilling marriage was to mourn a childhood that had been denied him and face the anger toward a father who abandoned him entirely and a mother who abused him. He did, in time, realize that as crazed and damaging as his mother's molestation was, the cause was her loneliness, her buried anger, and her complete lack of self-worth. Like Connie, he saw the power in the coping strategy, compassionate judgment, and he began to view understanding as a road toward forgiveness. As these events unfolded, Clyde became fully aware that his insights would improve the depth and quality of his professional commitments, and he felt profoundly grateful that he had found a professional life to fulfill him.

Social Burnout

The arena of our social relationships—from the most intimate relationships involving our partners and our immediate families to the outer concentric circles of friends and acquaintances—may be where the effects of our burnout are the most evident. Lashing out impatiently and harshly or the other extreme, rejecting loved ones by withdrawing, is more commonplace in our profession than most of us can bear to acknowledge and accept as inappropriate acting out, resulting from the exhaustion of burnout. It is surely also more commonplace than any of us desire. In the experiences of some of our respondents:

> When I come home after working all week, all I want to do is just sleep. I sometimes come home grumpy and upset, which takes a toll on my fiancé. He does his best to support me and give me encouraging words, but I know he gets tired of getting texts from me most nights about how I just want to walk out. (Respondent #24)

※ ※ ※

> Yes I have lashed out at loved ones from being burned-out. I would describe it as a low-frustration tolerance because I felt worn out and exhausted at times." (Respondent #60)

✳ ✳ ✳

Most poignantly, my family relationships have been affected the most because they are often not able to understand the extreme stress of holding space for such a complicated, hurting population. They try to be empathetic, but I think they lack an understanding for how much of my headspace it occupies at any given moment." (Respondent #21)

Another feature of social burnout is our inability to shift from being the source of trusted wisdom to our clients to being a mother, father, spouse, friend, son, or daughter and offering what these important relationships require. Our loved ones know us best, and if we are wise (and those who speak honestly to us about how we may be coming across can be trusted), we will see their words not as criticism or attacks but as examples of their care. The following is an example of this quality of honest feedback encompassing the important message: "Enough is absolutely enough!"

I became so used to the pedestal that my clients put me on that my boyfriend told me I was impossible to live with at home. In fact, he told me, "You are acting like God. Hey, you are great, but cut it out. You're human, just like me." I relayed this exchange to my supervisor, who then asked me: 'Do you think that your need to be on the pedestal keeps clients from telling you what they believe will disappoint you? Do you think that it also keeps you from confronting some pain during your own formative years?' (Respondent #49)

We may also consciously or unconsciously take this need for a pedestal, an idealized version of ourselves, to our social circle, with deleterious effects for all in the long run. The concept of role identity is an interesting one to consider here. As defined by Siebert and Siebert (2007), "Role identity is the character and role that a person devises as the occupant of a particular social position. This is an imaginative view, idealized, and includes standards of achievement and conduct that may not be consistently attained in day-to-day life" (p. 50). This means that friends or acquaintances may ask for our professional help and feedback in a social setting when we are looking forward to fun and relaxation for ourselves. We may feel compelled to do more than is ethically or realistically possible, draining ourselves and not offering the wisest feedback and counsel to those we care about.

My social work supervisee, Molly, lived in a neighborhood of professional couples, each in varied fields including medicine, law, social work, writing, and the media. Every other week, the couples, now close friends, shared a Friday evening potluck supper for themselves and their children. One Friday evening in December, Sophie arrived in an uncharacteristically disheveled state. Her hair was uncombed; her clothing was rumpled; her kids were without coats.

She immediately took Molly into a corner, broke down in tears, and told her that she needed help. She explained: "This morning Dennis (Sophie's husband) came into the kitchen as I was packing lunches and giving the kids breakfast. He told me that he had put his suitcases in the car when I was showering. He said he was leaving but would not tell me why. He also would not tell me where he could be reached and just walked out."

Following this evening, Sophie either texted or telephoned Molly at least twice a day, demanding answers about how things could have "gone so wrong." She would insist on receiving diagnoses: "What is wrong with Dennis?" "What is wrong with me?" Molly attempted to offer appropriate responses; she said how sorry she was that Sophie and the children were going through this, and she tried to share appropriate, general feedback about what she knew could go wrong in a marriage.

But Sophie could not be satisfied and demanded more and more from her. She began telling Molly about sexual frustrations in her marital life, asking for advice and feedback. Finally, Molly began to see that the direction the friendship was moving in was both inappropriate and exhausting. She was hearing details that were none of her business, ones that belonged in a counseling or therapy setting. Further, Molly realized that she was taking her role as social worker into her personal life and that this was leading her toward burnout in her workplace. "I just did not know how to say 'no' to a friend," she told me. "I feared letting her down so much."

Through this insight, however, Molly saw that it was, in fact, her lack of discretion regarding appropriate boundaries that was letting her friend down: "I needed to be needed much too much. Being needed made me feel safe and important, even powerful. It helped me to push down all of the hurt about how abandoned and alone I felt as a child. I feared losing a friend if I did not acquiesce to her demands and deluded myself that I was helping her."

Molly gave Sophie the name of three excellent family service resources. She said she would continue to help with the children whenever she could and in any way that she could. She assured Sophie that she would remain her friend but that the support and directions appropriate for counseling and therapy had to be found in these facilities.

Sophie's initial response was anger: "But you are a social worker, and you know me and all involved. You are more help to me than someone I do not know. How dare you walk away!"

But Molly held her own. Appropriate boundaries were respected, appropriate counseling was received, and the friendship between Molly and Sophie continued.

Physical Burnout

In the arenas we have looked at thus far, burnout flows from the professional to the personal and the social; that is, it originates in our work challenges and our difficulty adjusting to powerful stressors such as bureaucratic red tape or the inflexibility of supervisors. The effects are then felt in our internal worlds and in our social relationships with partners, friends, and family. In this directional flow, the last arena that burnout touches is that of our physical bodies. Because of the incapacitating nature of severe physical symptoms that may arise from burnout, we might say that the buck stops here.

A 2011 review of the literature found substantial evidence that physical illness resulted from burnout, including an increased likelihood of musculoskeletal disorders, cardiovascular diseases, somatic complaints, sleep disturbances, gastroenteritis, headaches, the flu, and common colds, all of which resulted in increased illness-related absences from work (Kim, Ji, & Kao, 2011, p. 259). The failure to understand the physical challenges that can be posed by the prospect of burnout or recognize the occurrence of burnout itself can lead to a compromised immune system. In this way, the physical body may be a readout of the burnout experienced in all of the other arenas treated in this chapter. We know that our physical capacities are a marriage of heredity/biology and all aspects of our environment. Some of us may have had distinct health diagnoses from a young age, which have continued. Others may have developed them at a later age. Sometimes, however, parts of our bodies give us signals that something is amiss that is not yet a serious illness but may become one. All of us would do well to recognize these signals or, put another way, recognize when our bodies talk to us.

There may be things in our professional world that we cannot "stomach," and our stomachs tell us this. There are situations that seem impossible to deal with, to carry, that seem to "break our backs," and our backs tell us this. There are nights when sleep is interrupted or will not come due to fear or sadness about the clients and families we are committed to help, or about something our work is touching in our own lives that has been difficult to face. There may also be headaches due to anger, and flu-like illnesses when our bodies seem to crash.

This said, we can never assume that physical symptoms are a result of burnout. Each of us must have regular medical exams and consultations as indicated. Information received from one's physical constitution can be confusing, and it cannot be stressed enough that all unsteadying symptoms always deserve full medical evaluation. As one of our respondents put it:

> It was hard to ascertain if it was 'burnout' or physical illness, because the symptoms were similar (difficulty sleeping, headaches, a persistent eye-twitch, an intermittent fever, and dizziness). . . . (This) outcome was actually physical illness, but the initial presentation was disinterest in work, fatigue, and that familiar sense of drudgery. (Respondent #2)

Working to your potential as a social worker or in any mental health concentration and taking care of yourself require balance. The motivation to accomplish this is born not only of the desire to take good care of our bodies for the sake of ourselves and our loved ones, but also from an awareness that if burnout affects our physical health it will in turn negatively affect each of the other arenas of our lives: professional, personal and social.

Erica had a brutal year. Her mother died, and her husband, Frank, was diagnosed with prostate cancer. To make matters more complicated, when this dual tragedy struck, Erica's daughter, an only child, was planning her wedding. Further, the social work department in the hospital where Erica had worked for 20 years was in the process of being totally reorganized. Several social workers were let go, and the focus of the work of the department was moving increasingly toward care management.

Social workers with strong backgrounds and competence working with cancer patients receiving various treatments and their families, as well as those on dialysis and their families, found their consults being shifted to the department of psychiatry, where residents with little experience became the new clinicians. Erica resented this shift and was exhausted from her innumerable responsibilities, fears, and disappointments; she ignored the occurrence of several physical symptoms, including nausea and vomiting, constant stomach pain, fevers and chills, a loss of appetite, and pain when she did eat.

A month before her daughter's wedding, Erica developed a bowel obstruction. Her doctor told her that she reached him just in time; had her bowel perforated, the infection could have killed her. Erica was facing challenges thrown at her all at once, ones that drained her, ones that, without professional help, she could no longer cope with, no longer "stomach." This quintessential wake-up call of burnout meant for Erica that therapy was necessary.

Through therapy, Erica realized how poorly she had been taking care of herself and that, despite the loss of her mother and fear for her husband's future, she had to live, to enjoy what she could. With a new positive attitude, Erica and her daughter began to concentrate on upcoming wedding plans and to enjoy this new collaboration enormously. Frank's therapy progressed well, and he found great pleasure in the delight of his wife and daughter. The couple was together and joyous as their daughter and son-in-law began their new life together.

However, there was more: Erica decided to make an appointment with the medical director of her hospital. She presented him, in writing, with a thorough documentation of what the hospital was giving up by excluding medical social workers in forthcoming treatment protocols as the hospital moved toward reorganization. Through this documentation and subsequent discussions, he realized that the body of hard-won social work knowledge concerning the care of patients and their families should not be lost. Under new health mandates, a large Accountable Care Organization for Medicare patients was being developed, one that physicians in her hospital were participating in. As a result of Erica's assertiveness, the medical director realized it was prudent and cost effective to assign Erica and her colleagues to help plan and coordinate this exciting initiative.

Questions for Reflection

Remember that although burnout may initially flow from the professional through the personal and social to the physical, once the experience of burnout has set in, it is an interdependent phenomenon: The symptoms may occur in any or all of the four arenas, and the relationships between the arenas can be both intricate and complex. Below are some questions for reflection to help you consider if burnout is operating in your life and, if so, in which arena or arenas—professional, personal, social, and/or physical—it is making its presence known.

- Does your organization encourage the discussion of burnout or offer opportunities for professional development in which you can learn more about how burnout affects you individually?
- Alternately, if you are in private practice or work with a small group, do you discuss burnout frankly and compassionately with your colleagues?
- Are your supervisors or your coworkers suffering from burnout? Do you recognize any of the signs mentioned in this chapter, or do you see others?
- How would you describe your internal experience at work? Do you feel ready and energized to accept your job's challenges? How do you know whether you are or are not in this state?

- You have read some of the common negative recurring ideations that result from burnout (for example, "I cannot make it through this day, I am failing my clients/a client in particular," and so on) Do you experience these thoughts? If so, what words and thoughts do you find yourself feeling or expressing?

- Do you find yourself recalling the commitment you made to the social work profession as a way to handle a difficult situation, day, or week? Do you do this as a reaction to feelings of burnout, or do you do this proactively?

- Have your relationships outside of the social work sphere been affected by burnout? Which ones, and how?

- Do you feel particularly susceptible to common illnesses such as colds, flu, and viruses? Are there times where there is something "going around," yet you are the only one who seems to be suffering from it?

- Are there other physical manifestations (lower back pain, neck pain, eye twitch, and so on) you experience during intense periods of work that continue to persist when the work intensity has lessened?

- Are there those important to you, inside or outside of mental health and related fields, who are experiencing the noted symptoms and reactions? Would opportunities for reflection be meaningful to them? If so, would discussion about mutual concerns be beneficial?

Chapter 3

From Compassion Fatigue to Compassion Satisfaction

By this point in the book, you have likely become convinced of the reality of burnout and its three attendant syndromes or faces: compassion fatigue, countertransference, and vicarious trauma. You have seen that burnout can be hard to accept on a fundamental level and is much more prevalent than most realize. This chapter will concentrate on the transition from compassion fatigue to compassion satisfaction, as well as the impediments to this process. There will be focus on the importance of empathy, which safeguards appropriate boundaries and protects the road toward this essential transition.

All of us have demanding lives, balancing many responsibilities. As we live and do our best to meet our responsibilities, it is very hard to pay attention to a warning voice within that tells us that "something" just is not right and that "something" may well be burnout. Often, it just feels easier—and more responsible to those we care about in both our personal and professional worlds—to push ahead, doing what we believe is expected of us. In the long run, however, this attitude can and will take an enormous toll.

Perhaps we do not want to think about what we are sensing, much less speak about it. Perhaps we know things like "exercise is good for me," but we do not know how to incorporate this knowledge into our lives. We may feel that we lack the self-care tools to bring what is necessary into our day-to-day lives.

Yet, we do have control in the matter of burnout. With awareness and insight about its vital importance, we can will ourselves to care for ourselves: We can convert compassion fatigue into what has been referred to in the literature as *compassion satisfaction* (Radey & Figley, 2007).

An in-depth understanding and appreciation of this vital transition will greatly enhance, and perhaps transform, our lives. One note: Of the three attendant syndromes of burnout described in this book, this chapter will focus on compassion fatigue as the most general or overriding consideration for social workers needing change. Although countertransference and vicarious trauma are very real aspects of burnout, each has a more specific purview; compassion fatigue, on the other hand, strikes everyone who is burned out without fail. Just as emotional abuse can exist independently but is always a component of physical and sexual abuse (Smullens, 2010), compassion fatigue exists wherever we see burnout that is a result of countertransference and vicarious trauma.

Compassion Satisfaction

The term "compassion satisfaction" was introduced in 2007 by Radey and Figley to describe the feelings of fulfillment social workers find when involved in their work helping others. The process of being present as our clients suffer less and transform from the role of victim to survivor allows us to reach professional fulfillment, as well as personal satisfaction (Radey & Figley, 2007). We instinctively know this to be true through our day-to-day experiences being there, bearing witness as our clients "do the work" to grow and change. As this transformation occurs, a social worker's feelings of "heart or soul sickness" dissolve.

Schwartz, Tiamiyu, and Dyer (2007) pointed out that, "Although most studies on burnout have focused on the negative and difficult aspects of social work, a few have advanced the idea that care-giving, itself, often has an intrinsically positive effect that can mitigate the stressors that otherwise lead to burnout" (p. 104). The research supports this: Compassion satisfaction, the positive feelings and pleasure social workers gain from our work, is positively associated with lower levels of burnout (Agllias, 2012).

Radey and Figley (2007) postulated a positivity-to-negativity ratio that helps us predict whether our daily input will lead us toward compassion fatigue or compassion satisfaction. The more we are able to maximize our positivity, which includes feeling grateful and upbeat and expressing appreciation, the greater our compassion satisfaction. On the other hand, negativity, represented by contemptuousness or irritability, leads to compassion fatigue.

It is understandable that pervasive negativity leads to and keeps us locked in a cycle of burnout, in which, according to Fox, "factors interact with each other to precipitate distress and consequent isolation; these reactions, in turn, exacerbate the negative consequences that are produced in us in the first place" (2003, p. 50). The relationship between compassion satisfaction and self-care, on the other hand, helps us avoid negativity altogether or return from it to positivity with such associated benefits as optimism and constructive problem solving: Feeling encouraged ourselves, we are then able to offer encouragement to others, but how do we know for sure in any given moment whether we are experiencing positivity or negativity? One way is to listen to ourselves and to be aware of the simple things we say to ourselves and others.

Recurring Expressions of Compassion Fatigue

Compassion fatigue, which proceeds from and is compounded by negativity, takes different forms for different practitioners based on their caseloads, personal history, level of experience and training, and choice of organizational venue (Bourassa, 2009). Although the components that make up compassion fatigue are varied and highly individual, Fox (2003) highlighted four main discussion subjects or means of expression that therapists who are suffering from burnout are apt to embody:

1. emotional exhaustion resulting from intense transactions
2. a profound sense of inability to help acutely distressed clients
3. cynicism arising from a lack of observable progress with difficult situations, and
4. isolation accompanying the absence of social support (p. 50).

Our respondents expressed the experience of compassion fatigue along very similar and somewhat overlapping lines, with the following five categories of negatively recurring ideations. (Note: you may have already read some of these quotations in previous chapters; they are reproduced here to share a sense of the overall picture.)

1. Clients are not making progress.

   "My clients are not making progress."
   "They're not going to succeed so why should I stress out?"
   "My client(s) will not get better."
   "There's nothing I can do to help this client."

2. I am failing my clients.

   "I'm going to fail this client."
   "I am not doing a good enough job."
   "I am not paying attention to everything I need to pay attention to."
   "I don't know how to change this."
   "I am not effective as a clinician."
   "I'm a terrible social worker."

Some combination of 1 and 2.

"I am not doing my best; therefore I am not providing quality care."
"I am not able to perform at my best, which impacts my clients."

3. Despair over the efficacy of social work.

"This work is hard."
"I just can't fix everything."
"Why bother?"
"I should have chosen a different profession."
"What difference are we really making?"
"What is the point if no one cares?"

4. Despair over the organization challenges in social work.

"I really need help with this and there isn't any."
"I'm not good at being a politician."
"I suck at supervising staff; why even try?"
"I could leave the office and no one would know."

5. The need for personal regeneration.

"I'll never catch up."
"It is a never-ending cycle."
"I need a break."
"When can I take some time off?"
"I cannot continue with this schedule."
"How can I help anyone else when I can't even help myself?"

You may find yourself resonating with one or more of the preceding statements. The questions for reflection at the close of every chapter present an opportunity to reflect further. You may also find it helpful to speak to a trusted partner, friend, colleague, mentor, or other adviser about your experiences. Even those not in a related field may wish to share their own feelings of negativity when life challenges and world events lead to what a respected friend has described as "general malaise, existential fear—a pervasive feeling of the blahs." Communication eases a feeling of aloneness and lifts spirits.

Still, even with those to confide in, share with, and feel encouraged by, it is exceedingly unsettling to hear so many deflating things about your chosen profession from others, especially when they resonate within yourself. Where could so much negativity be coming from? Can our framing of and reaction to our clients be part of the problem?

Establishing Proper Boundaries:
Pity, Sympathy, and Empathy

One of the main themes of this book is that burnout, as represented here by the draining negativity of compassion fatigue, is first and foremost a matter of establishing successful boundaries between ourselves and our clients. Undoubtedly, social workers are guided by compassion for others and a desire to improve individual and societal conditions (Radey & Figley, 2007). It is meaningful, fulfilling, and uplifting to see our clients grow and change.

However, one of our challenges is to make sure that our primary motivation must be this growth and change, not an escape from difficulties we have known ourselves or witnessed our loved ones endure and perhaps be destroyed by— and not a desire to have control or power over others to make up for what has been denied us or those we love. Without realizing it, many come into social work and related fields wanting to help others, needing to help others, but not primarily because of the client. As we have seen, many may be attracted to social work and related professions to escape from and compensate for their own pain or the pain of those they loved and needed, those who have let them down and disappointed them in myriad ways, sometimes callously and brutally. Simply put, many may be attracted to social work or related professions to soothe their own agonizing or traumatic life events and in this way find peace in their own lives. Though not aware of it, people's choice of a profession devoted to mental health may be attractive due to an urgent desire to ease distress regarding events in their own lives that have not been dealt with and understood.

This initial motivation is true for some of our most passionate and effective social workers, as well as those in related professions. In facing this hard truth, one is able to make the necessary shift in professional direction by realizing that we can never heal through our clients. Once we can clearly distinguish between our needs and the needs of our clients, we can more fully appreciate how essential appropriate boundaries are in our lives and work and to the vital connection to compassion satisfaction.

We call on the strengths and power of our professional relationships, which are the keys to our effectiveness in building mutual respect and trust. Sometimes we are the very first people our clients will learn to trust. The success of our work is most evident when a professional relationship can conclude—when a client, couple, or family (and for some in our profession, an organization or board) recognizes it is time to move forward independently with the confidence to define direction and face inevitable stress and frustration. With this achievement, we let go, ending our relationship—understanding and appreciating the success attained: A client's journey forward is his, her, or their own; we no longer are necessary for survival, sustenance, or direction. Without appropriate boundaries this process will be seriously impaired, and exhaustion, negativity, and fatigue will make professional satisfaction impossible to achieve.

Respectful boundaries are understood and valued through our own hard-won self-awareness and the professional confidence and autonomy it makes possible. Through an appreciation of the relationship between appropriate boundaries and what I think of as an effective "letting go/ending process," we understand that the term "helping professions" is perhaps a misleading one. We use our knowledge and skill to work with our clients for one reason: so that they are able to help and care for themselves and, through this ability, find personal direction and fulfillment in love, friendship, and work.

An understanding of the words "pity," "sympathy," and "empathy"—and their relationship to compassion satisfaction—is an effective way to conceptualize the difference between social workers who are motivated to escape their own feelings of pain and disappointments through their work and those who have learned to appreciate necessary boundaries for their work to be effective, for both their clients and themselves. (Please note: In the following discussion of pity, sympathy, and empathy, I draw largely on the research and work of Karen Gerdes [2011]. The integration of empathy and compassion that is discussed and its relationship to the Self are based on my own experience.)

Pity, sympathy, and empathy are three interlinked words in our lexicon. The first of these terms, "pity," is currently understood by our culture as "a condescending or contemptuous form of 'feeling sorry for' someone, often directed at people who are perceived as self-destructive or blameworthy" (Gerdes, 2011, p. 232). We can most likely see easily why pitying a client would be self-defeating. While pity originally had the positive connotation of being able to feel sorrow for another's suffering or misfortune, this has gradually morphed into the view of pity as a kind of moral high ground (Gerdes, 2011). Although this is clearly not what our clients need, a social worker or one in a related profession without self-awareness, drawn to the field to escape certain personal fears and truths, can easily and understandably pity a client as a way both to deny personal pain or panic and to feel stronger and safer. The unintended result of this adaptation is a guise of superiority and condescension. As an example, I have often heard those in medical and mental health settings leave an interview muttering, "Poor thing."

Sympathy, on the other hand, does not embody condescension or superiority. The word itself is derived from the Greek work prefix syn-, meaning "together" and the word pathos, meaning "feeling" (Gerdes, 2011, p. 232). This compound word designating fellow feeling then is very similar to our word compassion: com-, meaning "with" and passion, originally meaning "to bear" or "to suffer." According to Gerdes, sympathy then denotes "the immediate sharing of the same emotion with another . . . identifying with the feelings of another in reaction to the same external stimulus and understanding and respecting the emotional state of mind of another" (p. 233). To sympathize is to experience a heightened awareness as well as the integration of another's loss, pain, and agony; and we become deeply saddened by his, her, or their suffering. In a professional relationship, this expression of concern and sorrow about distressful events in another's life, while possibly laying the groundwork for a successful therapeutic intervention, can nonetheless eventually lead to dependency, codependency, or the hierarchy of entitlement, involving privilege and dispensation, whereas empathy—our third and final concept—can actually bring the client to empowerment, self-efficacy, and optimism.

In contrast to the terms "pity" and "sympathy," the concept of "empathy" is only about 100 years old. The main difference between empathy, on the one hand, and sympathy or pity, on the other, is that empathy reflects one's ability to erect and maintain boundaries. In a process such as social work, empathy represents the skill or disposition by which we can "perceive and feel the world from the subjective experience of another person" (Gerdes, 2011, p. 233). In this way, we can separate our life and its challenges from the lives and challenges of our clients. This is quite different from sympathy—the incorporation of an experience into our very being—which plants the seeds of compassion fatigue.

Although we may find it very difficult to develop empathy for all of our clients, it can remain a goal we always work toward. It is important to remember that the act of working toward this goal safeguards our own strength and, as Gerdes points out, is also the most effective avenue for the development of mutual trust and respect. Even if clients do not verbalize it, they may well experience pity as condescending and sympathy as invasive. Empathy, however, encourages a mutually respectful professional relationship to motivate growth, encourage insight and awareness, recognize options, and facilitate change. I think of it as a gift of Self to our clients as they work through loss and pain; address and clear up confusion; and identify individual paths toward self-respect, confidence, and autonomy. (In the next chapter, I will discuss the work of Otto Rank and his concept of Self.)

The force that sustains and protects empathy, perhaps best described as its engine or instrument of energy and strength, is compassion: an active, motivated, and passionate use of one's Self to alleviate the deep and anguished suffering of another. The success of each professional relationship—the heart, the core of our effectiveness—as well as our own well-being, depends on the interrelationship of empathy, the ability to perceive and understand the world of another without becoming part of it, and compassion, empathy's force and protector through the active use of one's Self, to motivate and cause productive change in another or others (and in ourselves). With use of *empathic skill*, a client can feel protected in the therapeutic state of being, knowing: "I am not a *thing*. I am human. I am not pitied. I am not patronized or condescended to. I will not be intruded upon, controlled, or devoured by another's neediness. I know I am respected, and I feel safe." Through professional *compassion*, a client feels the power of inner strength and the ability to change: "I feel hope. I am energized. I am beginning to believe in my Self and my ability to make or break my own life. I can change attitudes and see new options and possibilities. I can and will work hard to move forward."

The union of empathy and compassion can lead to transformative experiences, ones we are privileged to witness. Change and growth are a complex interrelated slow back-and-forth process. However, in this process, there also can be moments when client growth and change is immediately palpable, as if a lightning force has entered the room. Old imprisoning skin seems to begin to fall off, allowing new confidence, perspective, energy, and direction to emerge. This often happens when a client who has worked to become self-aware and appreciate mutual respect believes he or she has reached rock bottom but actually in his or her "fall" has discarded whatever was crippling capacities and blinding true vision. This marks the beginning of the birth of a new and healthy Self, marking a magical moment for both client and social worker.

The ability, perhaps the art, of achieving, maintaining, and protecting these described guiding delineations so necessary in our work rests with ever seeing our Selves as separate from our clients—knowing how to be there fully for them, give appropriately, but at the same time *care for ourselves*. As has been stressed, compassion is susceptible to deep and debilitating fatigue when self-care is not an integrated part of a social worker's life.

Positively Recurring Expressions of Compassion Satisfaction

We have seen how self-awareness leads to an appreciation of appropriate therapeutic boundaries; how empathy promotes mutually respectful and effective professional relationships, safeguarding these boundaries; and how compassion acts as the engine for and protector of empathy through active engagement to alleviate pain and promote growth and confidence. If compassion fatigue begins and is not recognized and addressed, protection of these professional safeguards is severely compromised and eventually collapses; negativity, and irritability, as well as contemptuousness and condescension will devour them.

This appreciation and understanding leads to our upcoming concentration on the necessity of self-care. As we proceed, it is important to remember that the flow between empathy/compassion and appropriate self-care is in essence a two-way street, an I/Thou relationship, each protecting the other as it protects all of us and our clients.

Put in a different way, self-care provides and protects the energy necessary to maintain compassion satisfaction, and vice versa. It helps maintain the emphasized appropriate boundaries and necessary flow so that empathy can flourish and compassion fatigue can continue to be lifted as well as avoided. Through this process, those in social work and related fields can continue to offer relationships to clients and coworkers that are effective, restorative, and powerful.

Some of the specific factors associated with maintaining compassion satisfaction are the very elements I will discuss in future chapters, where I will introduce the concept of the Self and its relationship to myriad self-care protectors, including social support, rest, and a greater sense of control at work.

The importance of an exploration of Self in this ebb and flow is vital, as effective self-care practices vary from individual to individual: While a certain combination works very well for one social worker, a different combination must be found for another. We must therefore judge our self-care efforts by their fruits, and these fruits can often be found most clearly in our recurring positive ideations. Just as we can become aware of our recurring negative ideations ("I am failing my clients," "I will never catch up") as a warning sign that we are approaching burnout, so certain positive expressions can point to a situation in which the intimate relationship between compassion satisfaction and self-care strategies is working effectively.

For the respondents, such positively recurring experience looked and felt like this:

"Nothing else stirs my passion like this job, so that helps me keep perspective."
"Balanced, nonjudgmental, patient, optimistic/hopeful."
"I (can) face my job's challenges through self-encouragement and encouragement from those who love and care about me."
"For me, it is refocusing on each day and focusing on one client at a time as much as possible. It is putting aside any personal issues and focusing on work."

"My mind is calm, not obsessed with solving a problem but ready to listen and explore gently. This calmness of mind is evidenced by a calm heart rate and relaxed neck and shoulder muscles."

"It's a feeling of strength and optimism. At this point in my career, I definitely know the difference between being up for the challenge or not, AND I am very clear about whether the challenge and the good I can potentially do are worth the 'output' involved."

"I feel relaxed and informed. I tend to feel like this after a positive staff meeting, where things are communicated effectively and problems are acknowledged."

"I feel inspired, motivated, creative and energized."

"I feel calm and ready to face the day."

"I feel clear."

From Compassion Fatigue to Compassion Satisfaction: A Case Study

Ellie and I began to work together when she was a second-year MSW student whose field placement was in a Veterans Affairs Medical Center. She was referred by her supervisor because of her difficulty working with a marine who had lost both legs in Iraq. Ellie frequently forgot that her client, Tony, had scheduled appointments with her, and she would have bouts of vomiting and severe intestinal pain after her sessions with him.

Tony, a star athlete in college, became engaged to his fellow student and childhood sweetheart, Dorothy, during their senior year. A gifted forward on his basketball team, as well as a fine student, Tony was sociable, confident, and exceedingly well liked and respected by students, faculty, and his coaches.. Soon after his college graduation, during the Second Gulf War, Tony felt it was his duty to enlist, wanting both to serve his country and help bring stability to a part of the world where suffering had been enormous and constant. Dorothy and he planned to marry when he returned from Iraq. In his second month in combat, as Tony tried to pull a wounded fellow soldier to safety, a blast from across enemy lines struck both of his legs. He was stabilized and shipped to a field hospital where, in order to save his life, above-the-knee amputations of both legs was necessary.

When Tony was returned to the United States, Dorothy was so stricken that she left visits with Tony early and then avoided them completely, writing him long letters expressing her anguish, her lost hopes, and her guilt about not being able to face him. Tony knew he had to learn to walk once again, but depression consumed and immobilized him.

By her second month of working with Tony, Ellie no longer forgot appointments. Her intestinal pain and vomiting episodes lessened, yet she was consistently late for their scheduled times together. In one session, when she made an excuse for arriving 10 minutes late, Tony began to shriek that he hated her for being sickened by him: "How dare you condescend to me?" he screamed. "I am still a human being. I am still a man. Stop avoiding me. Stop pitying me. I am here, and I am not dead."

Ellie sat, dazed and immobilized, as Tony wheeled himself from her office. She was too upset and shaken by Tony's rage and her own unfinished emotional business to realize that Tony was displacing his angst resulting from Dorothy's rejection on her. When Ellie told her supervisor the facts related to this episode but refused to discuss its impact on her, Ellie's supervisor urged her to do so during her next appointment with me.

At first, Ellie would not speak to me about this either. In time, however, I learned that Ellie had been an only child whose father, an alcoholic, abandoned his wife and daughter when Ellie was 10. Ellie never saw her mother know happiness, and a year after her father left their small, vulnerable family, her mother committed suicide. Ellie was raised in foster care, where she bonded with her third foster family and was adopted.

Ellie had worked hard to grow up and stay strong and positive. Her way to accomplish this was to push her devastating years from her mind and to determinedly keep them there, isolated, as if walled away by an cast-iron barrier. Ellie had been happily married for four years when we met, and she and her husband were planning to begin a family. Her adoptive parents and two older sisters were very close to the young couple. But, as was inevitable in the work Ellie had chosen, the barrier that protected her from past rage and terror would crumble through a client's truths. In one session with me during our fourth month of work together, Ellie began to cry hysterically and then to scream, "Both of my parents were cripples. Both gave up. Both left me. No fight in them, the damned cripples!"

Through her outburst, Ellie realized that her past traumas began to come to consciousness as soon as she met Tony. She also realized how insistently she tried to keep them far away by distancing herself from her client. She understood that rather than face and mourn the losses endured in her youth, she had, in her words, "buried them" and that only by fiercely holding on to this pretense did she feel able to move forward in her life. Through this truthful outburst, Ellie's pretense was pierced, and she was finally able to begin to face her own intense pain, terror, and loss. By working through these personal truths, Ellie felt as if, in her words, "my own crippling blockage of pain, terror, and rage carried throughout my life has finally been lifted." She realized further, "My new freedom isn't only in my work. It is in my life."

Through this process, Ellie, for the first time, was able to know empathy and feel it in her relationship with Tony. She realized that Dorothy also needed a safe place to mourn her loss brought on by Tony's injuries. Ellie, through her own insights, realized that Dorothy would never see things clearly and make necessary decisions in her own life until this was accomplished and an appropriate referral was made. Dorothy's terror left her, and Tony's depression lifted. A gifted athlete, Tony adjusted to the necessary prosthesis required for each leg, and within six months he was once again on his beloved basketball court. Before that, he and Dorothy were married—and yes, as you may have guessed, not long after they married, Ellie gave birth to their first child.

Questions for Reflection

Making the transition from compassion fatigue to compassion satisfaction is rarely a neat or easy process. The first thing to assess is where you are at the present time, on a daily, weekly, and monthly basis. The questions below are designed to help you assess where your negative and positive ideations concerning your career as a social worker truly lie. (Please note: References in the following questions to a "voice within" will be explained fully in chapter 4. Until you read further, think of this "voice" as a truth within yourself that is asking for your attention.)

- Do you experience recurring negative feelings that, regardless of your efforts, your clients are not making progress? When do these feelings occur? Can you translate them into a voice within? What is being said?
- Do you experience recurring negative concerns that you are not doing your best as you work with certain clients and are thus inhibiting their growth? Can you define the characteristics and challenges of these clients? Are these clients reminiscent of anyone in your past or current life?
- Do you find yourself despairing either over the effectiveness of social work in general or over the challenges you face in your particular organization? What areas are you most likely to feel overwhelmed by or powerless to address effectively?
- Do you experience the need for personal regeneration as a negative; that is, do you feel shame or guilt that you need to take care of yourself, or bitterness that it is not easier to do so in your current environment?

- How would you describe the internal experience of being ready to accept and confront your job's challenges? How do you know when you are in a positive state of mind?
- Are there those important to you, either in mental health or related fields or not, who are overwhelmed by dissatisfaction with their responsibilities? Would the questions noted be meaningful for them to also consider? Would discussion of their concerns and yours be beneficial?

PART 2
Self-Care

Chapter 4
Introducing Self-Care

In part 2 of this book, having explored the essential interactive relationship between compassion satisfaction and self-care, we will concentrate specifically on self-care as the antidote to the burnout that so many social workers and those in related fields face in their lifetimes. The categories of self-care will be well known to you as they are responses to the four categories of burnout examined to this point: professional self-care, personal self-care, social self-care, and physical self-care.

Before we begin a more in-depth study of self-care, however, the point must be made that most of what is described in the self-care literature is the "care" component: those behaviors, attitudes, and types of relationship that nurture us as social workers and those in related professions. There are many to consider. To name just a few: We can meditate; we can have a well planned and productive peer counseling meeting with our coworkers; we can go to the gym; and we can explore leisure options that have nothing to do with social work. Further, we can engage in those self-care approaches that may not hold appeal but that we know are good for us, ones we can learn to tolerate and perhaps even enjoy. In addition, we can create self-care approaches that are "out of the box" yet meaningful to us.

But what of the "self" that we are caring for? What is this self that we are trying to support through our self-care efforts? There are myriad ways to define and describe the self; a wide-ranging discussion of the emergence and development of this concept is, of course, beyond the scope of this book. It is possible to discuss the self through the expressions of art, such as poetry and prose, theatre, dance, films, and architecture, or through one's own religious preference. There are also numerous psychosocial approaches that concentrate on the essence of self, some of which do and some of which do not use the specific term "self." What is essential is that each of us form an individual conception of the self—one's own way to look at it to understand its importance and to make it work to proceed to care for this self, *our Self*. Each personal definition of self can be as fully dimensional and unique as the strategies used to take care of each Self—yours, mine, each of ours.

With this in mind, I present one discussion of Self by sharing a definition and its evolution that has worked effectively in my life and benefited my work with clients for over 30 years. My training at the University of Pennsylvania School of Social Work (now the University of Pennsylvania School of Social Policy and Practice) was based on the teachings of Otto Rank, a member of Sigmund Freud's initial Viennese Circle, which began in 1902. A sociologist, Rank was the only non-physician included in this esteemed and select gathering. He was also its youngest member. Rank's painful break with Freud, leading to his exclusion from the group, occurred as Rank's thinking evolved in ways that angered his powerful mentor (Lieberman, 1985).

To Sigmund Freud, a mature ability to love and work necessitated growing beyond the inner, unconscious turmoil and conflicts of the Oedipal complex, where children become rivals for the attentions of their opposite-sex parent, thus sparking an intense rivalry with their same-sex parents (whom they nonetheless strive to emulate). As his own work matured, however, Otto Rank grew to believe that there was another essential issue confronting each individual. In his paper, "The Trauma of Birth," published in 1929, Rank described this seminal issue as separation from mother, which then became "a prototype for all anxiety" (Lieberman, 1985, p. 221). Rank believed "separation anxiety" was the most important hurdle an individual had to face repetitively in his or her struggle to reach maturity and to live productively and well.

Psychologically, according to Rank, what was separated from the mother at birth, through a terrifying process for the newborn, was the infant's Self, replete with special internal power. Though strongly aware of the unconscious, Rank's clinical work did not focus primarily on those unconscious forces within each of us or their potentially destructive implications. Rather, he emphasized the importance of choice and self-determination, firmly believing that all individuals have the power to direct their own lives through an impassioned life force. Rank referred to this inner force as *Will*, defining it as "the integrative power of the self" (Lieberman, 1985, p. 402). Further, Rank believed that within each of us there is an "artist," whom I define as the embodiment of our individual *emotional sense of direction* (Smullens, 2003), one that becomes strong and reliable through hard-won insights and self-awareness. The artist, according to Rank, is our own unique creative guide, one that, if recognized and freed, can move us toward the life journey that is right for us. Using this perspective, each of us can value and rely on our own unique inner voice, our artist within, to guide us toward necessary insights, awareness, choices, and direction and in doing so protect us from the ravages of burnout. Thus, Rank became the first psycho-analyst to develop "a more optimistic view of the human race that conceived of individuals to be the creators of themselves" (Turner, 1986, p. 49).

The Self, as defined by Otto Rank, is living and unique. To be fulfilled, one must respect its life, its passion, and define its individual, unique direction. It must also be protected. Recognizing that to most fully enhance a helping pro-cess, a clinician must use his or her Self on behalf of the client—and acknowl-edging that therapy is a two-way street—Rank introduced an interactive, eclectic form of therapy that prefigured many approaches to follow, such as the client-centered therapy of Carl Rogers (Kramer, 1995). In Rankian interaction between client and clinician, the clinician received permission to become his or her real self in interaction with the client (Polster & Polster, 1974). It became okay to say, "Here's what I'm thinking (or feeling) as you talk," or, "As you described what happened, I could actually picture you as a child," or, "Do you remember a similar situation you described last week?" This approach allowed a new world of clinical possibilities.

From the point of view of burnout, however, this innovation offers a mixed blessing. As clinicians began using more of their selves when assisting and sup-porting clients, it became evident that this interactive approach (which many of us take for granted today) can also bring about exhaustion, contributing to some of the dangers associated with burnout.

As discussed previously, the heart, the core, of what social workers and those in related professions bring to our work is the quality of relationship we offer our clients. This relationship is strengthened by our academic knowledge, our self-awareness, and our life experience. To work effectively, we must under-stand the importance of always remembering that our clients are not there for us. The opposite is true: We are there for our clients. In expressing ourselves, our goals (as Rogers' formulation aptly puts it) are client centered; we are there for the client's needs and growth (Rogers, 1974). Conversely, a client-centered approach also allows a clinician or therapist to constructively and confidently challenge one who is not using what is offered to move forward or is not treat-ing a professional relationship respectfully.

Viewing our clients through this Rankian lens is a constant reminder of appropriate boundaries in the mutual give-and-take in a professional relation-ship. This is the reason that I capitalized the word "Self" in one of my previous books, *Setting YourSelf Free: Breaking the Cycle of Emotional Abuse in Family, Friendships, Work and Love*, where the importance of InnerSelf Dialogue is emphasized as the road toward insight, awareness, and change. A capitalized use of the word "Self" implies a completion, a separateness, an ability to care for and love through being whole, and not expecting another to fill in the missing parts of YourSelf. It is an understanding of and respect for boundaries that have been discussed throughout this book. This boundaried use of the Self is appropriate, encouraging professional involvement that leads to insight, reevaluation, and change. It is this full understanding of one's Self that helps social workers and those in related fields provide appropriate feedback, such as:

"I know what you stated as your goals, but I don't see you working to change to improve your life. Can we work together to understand why?"

"Let's look together at the positives in your life? What positives are visible to you? Are there positives you do not see or that you frame as negatives?"

"What are you going to do to free yourself from your pessimism and negativity?"

"I'm not just here to listen. I want to be with you as you reassess and alter behaviors and attitudes and work through the conflicts that are keeping you muddled and stuck in negativity."

"What are you going to do to make your life work?"

"Are we wasting your time, my time, and your money?"

Understanding that we will be using our Selves in our work is therefore fundamental to our understanding of the concept of self-care as we explore its many essential components. That this is the natural starting point for discussions of self-care can be seen in some of the recent discussions of burnout now going on in graduate-level social work. One such course, "Foundation Social Work Practice," at the University of Louisville phrased one of its objectives this way: "to enable students to critically understand how to make appropriate use of self" (Moore et al., 2011, p. 547).

According to Dewane (2006), this appropriate use of self, which is a hallmark of skilled practice, is achieved by "melding the professional self of what one knows (training, knowledge, techniques) with the personal self of who one is (personality traits, belief systems, and life experience)" (quoted in Taylor & Cheung, 2010, p. 160). In this way, the personal Self and the professional Self become one, where the personal *is* the professional and the professional *is* the personal. The results of such a successful integration can be profound, including "improved relationship-building skills, reduced anxiety, enhanced cultural competence, enhanced ethical practice, reduced burnout, and improved practice competency" (Taylor & Cheung, 2010, p. 162).

The logical extension of this integration is political expression of social work values on behalf of our clients, also an important self-care alternative. Just as social workers know that if the meek ever inherit the earth they would not have it very long, we also know that life is neither fair nor just, and it is up to each of us to make it as fair and just as it possibly can be. We also, of course, know that fairness and justice, as well as equality of opportunity, are far easier for some to attain than others. It is restorative when a social worker's professional Self—with an integrated respect for boundaries and appreciation for empathy and compassion—channels frustration, disappointment, and anger into thought-ful expressions of political assertion on behalf of our clients and our profes-sion. Thus, in our profession, the personal, professional, and political Selves are inextricably woven and become one. Put in a different way: The personal *is* the professional *is* the political—each intricately assimilated with the other. This assimilation allows the selection of effective self-care options and expressions of caring to facilitate hope, awareness, safety and opportunity.

The more we are able to use social work settings for appropriate professional expression of our complete professional Selves, the more we are able to bring hope to those who consult us, whose opportunities have been deeply limited, as well as to strengthen our own capacities to rebuff burnout, and if we do see those symptoms, do something about it. In future chapters, we will also exam-ine opportunities for this quality of full expression beyond our work settings. All of the successful self-care strategies that we will discuss have consolidated, multifaceted purposes: Our personal well-being is essential. Our appreciation of the necessary boundaries to enhance empathic capacity and expressed com-passion in our work with clients is essential. Also essential is a commitment to educate and inform about the necessity of a healthier, more equitable society (and the dangers to all if this necessity is disregarded) and, to the extent pos-sible, to work toward this fulfillment to our fullest capacities.

Now that we have seen how an understanding of the full professional Self is related to the concept of self-care, we can move forward to a discussion of the practices of self-care, from both a broader and a more detailed perspective.

Aspects of Self-Care

When we decide to strive for self-care in the field of social work, we immedi-ately find a difficulty in defining the term itself. Lee and Miller (2013) noted that while many have offered definitions of self-care, no consensus exists around any one conceptualization. Some authors of scholarly works on the sub-ject even omit a definition altogether, perhaps because they believe the meaning is explicit; that is, self-care means caring for oneself. Yet, just as the Self needs some consideration, so does the term "self-care." What are we striving for when we undertake self-care? How will we know when we have succeeded?

Moore et al. (2011) posited that self-care enhances well-being and agreed with Ashford, LeCroy, and Lortie's (2006) definition of *well-being* as "a person's emotional and psychological capacity to cope with demands across time, circumstance, and setting" (p. 530). Well-being so defined is largely a subjective experience, and with this in mind, it makes sense that the behaviors, activities, and relationships that help one attain well-being would be unique to any given social worker. This subjectivity is another challenge involved in first defining and then categorizing the concept of self-care.

In an effort to counter the subjectivity inherent in the practices of self-care, some researchers in the field have gone in the opposite direction and attempted to graft an objectivity onto self-care activities that I do not believe serves us well. For example, McGarrigle and Walsh reported that "Writing self-reflective journal entries and consultative discussions with colleagues have been suggested as ways for social workers to 'know self.' . . . There is however, a lack of evidence as to the effectiveness of these strategies" (2011, p. 215). This assertion will be countered in chapter 6, where effective uses of journaling will be offered, including documented positive experiences involving social work students.

The important thing to consider at this point is that when choosing your self-care strategies, research is important, but not everything can be measured. There are certain personal truths for you and others that research will not bring to light. For example, my experience is that my journaling has led to my writing, and my writing has led to my publishing. Throughout this dimension of self-care, I have been able to communicate to a broader audience, but in addition, as I have recorded my thoughts and process notes, exploring what I feel, believe, and have learned, I have grown in the depth of understanding my clients, my profession, and myself.

To continue our exploration of the complexity of the self-care discussion: Theorists have not even been able to conclusively identify what category of human endeavor self-care falls into. Some have described it as a process, and some describe it as an ability, whereas most describe it as an engagement in particular behaviors that have been suggested to promote specific outcomes, such as well-being (Lee & Miller, 2013).

I believe it is most effective to discuss self-care as a set of strategies (Norcross, 2000) that, while occasionally falling under the headings of attitudes or relationships, most easily are considered as a roster of behaviors or selective gifts to the Self, ones I consider to be necessary.

It may be going too far to describe self-care behaviors as "any activity that one does to feel good about oneself" (Lee & Miller, 2013, p. 97) because self-care must also effectively prevent and decrease burnout in the areas of the personal, the professional, the social, and the physical. Nonetheless, there is an inescapably subjective aspect of self-care that is bolstered by empirical reality. In other words, if it is working for you, it is working. Here again, we see the importance of the essential interaction of your Self and your care, and the importance of your allowing your unique artist within to be your guide. Please do not ever let another dissuade you from an expression of self-care that you feel excited or passionate about. Try what feels right to you. In your selections, there are no mistakes to be made; there are only learning experiences. It will become very clear whether something you try is not working for you; and in this case, there is only one thing to do: give it up and try something else.

As indicated in the previous chapter (in which recurring negative ideations prompted by compassion fatigue transitioned to the positive ideations expressive of compassion satisfaction), we as individuals must judge our self-care activities first and foremost by their effects on our lives. We each must come to appreciate the fine line between activities that build empathy and resilience, the ability to adapt despite threatening circumstances (Tosone, Minami, Bettman, & Jasperson, 2010), and those that appear enjoyable but whose frivolity is actually draining rather than replenishing. Remember throughout your self-care selections that anything that puts you more in touch with yourself, gives you a way to express the difficulties and frustrations you are experiencing, and helps you connect positively with other human beings is an extraordinarily meaningful self-care gift to YourSelf. There are some things you simply do not have to test in a laboratory. The wisest approach is to learn to trust, again calling on Rankian explanation, the voice of the singular guide within.

Recognizing that Self-Care Behaviors Are Transitory

If we are to define self-care as a set of behaviors, we must appreciate that these behaviors will be impermanent. If a self-care activity helps you on a given day, that's good enough. As one respondent explained, "I think the positive effects are transitory, but are required maintenance for a healthy professional perspective in the field of social work" (Respondent #60). Moore et al. believe that self-care does enhance well-being but only through "*purposeful and continuous efforts* that are undertaken to ensure that all dimensions of the self receive the attention that is needed to make the person fit to assist others" [italics added] (2011, p. 545).

One respondent addressed the constant threats of burnout in a way that recognizes that self-care is an individualized collection of practices that must become integrated into a social worker's life with constancy:

I practice yoga semi-frequently, which is very effective in helping me find balance. I go to the gym regularly to relieve work stress. The effects typically last for a day to several days depending on the circumstances. The effects of yoga last the longest. When I practice[d] weekly yoga, [it] kept me focused and balanced. (Respondent #70)

Social work vitality and stamina, through the use of self-care, require the kind of constant work that true gardeners offer their creations. Our gardens, however, are inner ones. These gardens require the same kind of dedication that devoted gardeners everywhere know well: Gardens must continually be visited, replenished, tended to. Because weeds with the power to destroy all we hold dear will easily invade what we have worked so hard to create, it is essential to remain consistently aware of their danger and the necessity of their removal. As social workers, we have *three gardens* to maintain: (1) *our personal inner garden*, (2) *the garden of our profession*, (3) *and their combination.*

To safeguard our personal inner garden, each of us must constantly protect ourselves from our own repetitive depleting patterns of behavior and attitude due to past life experiences involving personal pain, loss, rejection, and poor choices; and we must maintain the behaviors and attitudes to keep these weeds from destroying what we have worked hard to build for ourselves and those we love.

Our second garden involves the work we have chosen. The settings where we work may be inadequate, or we may lack good supervision. When these stresses are not addressed in positive ways that lead to change within an institution, colleagues who turn to each other for clarification, discussion, support, and decisions regarding appropriate direction and expression can help protect their energy and well-being.

In addition to insensitivities permeating our work settings, we live at a time when our society appears hopelessly divided and overwhelmingly heartless. Sensitivity to the poor and suffering through necessary funding of needed programs is at a premium. There are those convinced that government resources should not be used to protect the neediest and most vulnerable among us. Given these harsh attitudes, it is predictable that weeds of burnout will appear within us and, given the opportunity, flourish. We must recognize them determinedly and pull them out through available and effective self-care options.

Our third garden involves the overlap of the first two. We must know if a client who rejects our efforts is touching a loss in our personal life. We must be able to pull the weeds of past rejection and learned fear of anger that can appear, seemingly out of nowhere, if a client decides to leave our work without warning before change has occurred and has not or will not discuss why. We must deal with an obtuse supervisor or colleague as one different from a parent or sibling who treated us with contempt and unkindness. We must learn, to the best of our ability, to differentiate between a client outburst that signals a danger to himself, herself, or others (such as a direct threat that must be reported) and those cries for help indicating exhaustion, frustration, the need to express pent-up rage, an aching need for more support, or a combination.

This differentiation can present a fine line, for there are times, even when a client does not directly threaten another or others, when, to again use Rankian terms, our "inner voice" will warn that something may be terribly wrong. If this occurs, "our inner voice" should be trusted, and consultation about direction from an experienced supervisor or consultant becomes imperative immediately. Of special concern is a client who becomes angry or deeply depressed by change in his or her life or rejection of any sort, in either a personal or a professional sense, and expresses the urgency to be known, remembered, and famous. Stated simply, believe in the warnings you feel. Do not ignore them. When in any doubt about a client's capacities to function without endangering himself, herself, or others, get consultation immediately.

Further, we are proactive and wise to regularly examine what clients' intensely felt expressions touch in us about our own lives. With this discernment, all highly charged communication, including those personal and professional decisions made by our clients (that we wish had been different), lose their power to undermine or overwhelm our strength and confidence. They become the opposite—opportunities to reflect, understand, and determine appropriate direction and means of expression and move forward with confidence. This framing is also vital when dealing with administrative insensitivities.

Self-Care Conditions: Time, Permission, and Place

In chapter 5, we will move further into a discussion of individual self-care strategies within the four arenas of the professional, the personal, the social, and the physical; however, before we do, I want to address three more variables to be considered when approaching self-care: time, permission, and place. These three components were first identified and isolated by McGarrigle and Walsh (2011), and they resonate strongly with the material supplied by our respondents.

Having the time to practice self-care strategies has been identified by McGarrigle and Walsh as critical to practicing self-care and wellness, in terms of both having and taking time to implement self-care strategies. Having the time and taking the time are not the same thing of course, and moving from the former to the latter involves *permission* to commit to an individualized program of self-care. As social workers, our pledge to help others may misguide, causing us to withhold this permission from ourselves. Again and again, I have heard, "There is not enough time in the day to meet all the demands of my work. How can I possibly take time for me?" Those who are self-employed may also hesitate to engage in self-care strategies due to the pressures of financial well-being, actually fearing time away from the office, especially if some clients cancel or "next week looks a little thin."

For individuals who want to practice self-care in an organizational setting, time and permission usually depend on others. When such time and permission is given for coworkers to engage in self-care activities, however, the effects can be doubly effective. For example, a few respondents reported that the reality of burnout was an ongoing conversation within their current workplace. Another noted, "My program will sporadically allow for additional time outside of our weekly treatment team to support one another, especially when we have particularly emotionally draining cases" (Respondent #58). Such permission most often comes from one's supervisor and can take the form of one-on-one meetings, peer support, and trainings. One of our respondents brought together the need for time and permission, along with the need to establish proper boundaries for the most appropriate use of her Self this way:

My supervision towards my LCSW is overwhelmingly supportive of my burnout and need for time to myself. It is through that permission that I've been able to take time and feel less guilty about taking earned time during days when I normally see particular clients. It is an ongoing exercise to remind myself that my presence is not wholly responsible for their well-being. (Respondent #21)

The third self-care condition is that of *place*. In their study of a dozen human service workers, McGarrigle and Walsh (2011) reported that the positive outcomes associated with self-care strategies were more likely to occur at work. Since the effects of burnout are felt most keenly at work, many of our respondents agreed that one's work setting was the natural place to practice self-care. Unfortunately, for the vast majority of our respondents, this commitment to self-care was not shared by the organizations that employed them. In certain rare cases, one of their institutions set aside a dedicated place for self-care, such as in the experience of this respondent:

After much lobbying our hospital set aside a separate break room for the social workers on duty to use where we could relax and de-stress. I would say we took that ball and ran with it as we drew up a calendar of whose week it was to stock the fridge or bring in additional touches such as a great quote for the bulletin board or a humorous book that has nothing to do with social work. Knowing we have this place of respite has made going to work much, much easier. (Respondent #49)

Whenever possible, wise professionals do what we can to provide this place of respite within one's personal office space, where we spend more daytime hours than we do in our homes. A garden metaphor is also applied in the work of Skovholt, Grier, and Hanson (2001), who speak of "creating a professional greenhouse at work" (p. 174). This involves decisions such as the resolve to eat lunch alone at one's desk as little as possible; an appreciation of the importance of social exchange, as well as a comfortable chair; use of calming music as background for writing and thinking; and taking plants to your office. (A personal aside about plants: I well know that forgetting to water them is a sure wake-up call that your proactive self-care "gifts to YourSelf" are seriously lacking!)

Self-Care Strategies: A Case Study

My supervisee Natalie knew the importance of exercise to self-care and good health. But every time Natalie worked out, as much as she prepared with proper warm-up, she hurt her back, her neck, her leg, her something. She even injured an arm in Pilates, an experience she and her friends could find humor in, as the injury was not a serious one. She tried repeatedly, but never successfully, to find a physical self-care strategy that could fit in with her busy training schedule, which included having limited travel time to and from her workout destinations.

Finally, Natalie decided that she would rely on ballroom dancing for her exercise. She and three good friends laughed heartily as they struggled to learn the steps and pair up with available partners to execute the dance moves. Eventually, however, this experience led Natalie deeper into experiments with a wide variety of forms of dance. In Natalie's words:

The music is crucial to getting away, escaping to a different world of fun and outlet, one where I absolutely do not know what I am doing. But the sense of mastery when I do finally get the hang of certain steps that make up certain dances bolsters my confidence in myself and my courage to return to work and do my best.

Natalie's experience made me think of the words of a wise teacher in my life: "The animals in the jungle who survive know well that if one way does not work, they must find another. They do not keep banging their heads against the same walls, determined to get through. They find their individual ways to reach their destinations that work well for them." To this I add: One positive experience surely leads to another, if we allow the artist within each of our Selves to be our guide.

Questions for Reflection

Below are some questions for reflection about self-care activities in general before we turn to some chapters that are more specific in nature.

- How do you define your "Self" in terms of the full person you bring to work on your best days?
- Without fully knowing the full range of activities that you may engage in for self-care, can you begin to list those behaviors that lessen stress and build resilience at work? At home? When you are out with friends or family?
- Without fully knowing the complete range of activities that you engage in for self-care, can you estimate how much time you currently take for these practices in a given week?
- Do you engage in these activities during the workday, or are these activities solely reserved for after or before work or on the weekend?
- How do you feel about giving yourself permission to engage in self-care activities? Do such actions feel uncomfortably luxurious, or at another extreme, selfish? Or do you see them as essential to your continuing to function well as a social worker?
- Does your employer (if you are not self-employed) encourage self-care activities through your organization? Do you take advantage of these activities? If so, which do you find enjoyable and meaningful?
- Are there those important to you, either in social work and related professions or not, who you see are not caring for themselves or others? Would the past questions and opportunities for reflection be meaningful to them? Would sharing your experiences and concerns in your life, and asking them about their own, be beneficial?

Chapter 5
Professional Self-Care

In this chapter, we will look at three elements of professional self-care: self-care within or sponsored by an organization or institution; self-care in relationship to a seasoned professional, such as a supervisor or mentor; and self-care that is shared among peers or coworkers. These delineations will blend into each other, of course, just as professional self-care can blend into personal self-care, social self-care, and so on. For our focus, we will concentrate on professional self-care as that which takes place either in the workplace directly or closely related to the workplace. This includes enriching activities that colleagues share, such as attending conferences, taking continuing education classes, or reading about the subject of burnout and becoming educated about it. Social workers may be surprised to realize that learning about burnout is in itself an example of self-care. As one of our respondents put it:

> I went to a conference on compassion fatigue. At the time I did not realize
> I was experiencing burnout. However, just being at the conference listen-
> ing to people say what they really felt was cathartic. It felt so good to know
> that there are others out there (who) are going through what you are going
> through. (Respondent #16)

When self-care opportunities are not provided through an organization, supervision or mentoring, or accessible sharing with coworkers and peers, there are other avenues of compensation to explore: NASW helps both nationally and locally through publications that address all aspects of social work practice and research. Further, this devoted professional organization provides the latest information about licensing; offers social work conferences; endorses other courses; offers information about involvement in community initiatives; and provides rich opportunities for concentrated learning, networking, publishing, and further certifications. For those in clinical social work, many cities have highly successful clinical societies that supplement this ongoing commitment through innovative activities. Graduate schools of social work offer excellent continuing education and networking experiences, as well as further degrees and certifications. Both the American Group Psychotherapy Association and the American Association of Marriage and Family Therapy, as well as their local chapters, provide opportunities for engrossing workshops, courses, research, and further certification. Social work students can also learn about family life education certification offered by the National Council on Family Relations. Family life education, like marriage and family therapy, group therapy, and community organization/public and social policy concentration, has exceedingly strong roots in social work; and the exceptionally well-developed evidence-based family life education materials can complement and enhance social work process.

Organizational Support

The potential that an organization or institution has to both prevent and address the burnout of its social workers cannot be underestimated. Employment settings that engage and promote activities that encourage emotional health and satisfaction in the workplace can vastly improve the well-being and work functioning of their employees, These opportunities include increasing the amount of paid time off; starting support groups to manage work-related stress; increasing funds for professional development; and providing specific training on compassion fatigue, burnout, and self-care (Alkema, Linton, & Davies, 2008).

As I noted in the last chapter, receiving self-care in the same milieu in which the exposure to burnout has occurred—that is, the workplace—has a uniquely assuaging effect. An organizational culture that normalizes the effect of our difficult work is thus able to provide a supportive environment for social workers to more effectively address the effects of burnout in their own work and lives (Bell et al., 2003). By acknowledging the very real possibility of burnout, any ill-founded stigma attached to exhaustion, depletion, and lack of energy is removed. In high-functioning workplaces, burnout is discussed continually and is never seen as a sign of weakness.

There are further policy initiatives, in addition to encouraging employees to participate in continuing education and further training opportunities, that an organization can introduce to help ensure self-care within its walls. A supportive organization, for example, is one that not only allows time for vacations, but also insists that employees take advantage of their accumulated time off. The belief that not using accrued vacation time is a positive indication of a hardworking, valuable employee is a dated and debilitating concept. The opposite is now known to be true: Those unable or unwilling to use all of their vacation time have a higher incidence of heart attacks, long-term disability, and death from a variety of stress-related diseases such as type 2 diabetes (Burke & Cooper, 2008). It is likewise a dated expectation that, even when ill, workers are to be present at their places of employment. Rather than demonstrate that such an individual is a motivated employee, this behavior underscores the obvious: An ill employee cannot concentrate and thus decreases productivity, puts others at risk, and compromises the effectiveness of medications he or she may be taking.

An essential part of organizational support is a social worker's physical safety. The risks of personal injury and even death of social workers due to violence has been widely reported. Of course, this is true in other related fields as well; however, some social work sites, such as shelters or hospitals, can be located in high-crime neighborhoods that are so dangerous workers may experience primary traumatization as well as vicarious trauma (Bell et al., 2003). With this awareness, social workers must be assured a safe work environment. There are times when hiring outside consultation regarding safety management and provisions is a necessity. Further, there are settings that require the presence of police or hired security personnel.

Beyond the immediate physical environment, an organization that can offer variety and diversity within its walls is one that is likely to reduce burnout. Research has shown that having a more diverse caseload is associated with reduced burnout (Chrestman, 1995). Rotations in which a social worker changes focus—such as moving from direct care to a traumatized population to participating in social change activities—may also be of benefit (Regehr & Cadell, 1999). In fact, any form of diversity can help social workers keep tasks and engagements in perspective, becoming more able to buffer the trauma to which they are exposed and, in this way, avoid forming what Pearlman and Saakvitne (1995) described as a "traumatic worldview."

Regardless of one's field of endeavor, flexibility and taking advantage of creative opportunities are hallmarks of a well-functioning individual. With this in mind, to become less depleted, social workers may want to take advantage of an opportunity to change their routine, such as leading a group instead of engaging in individual therapy on a given work day, or offering a family life education course to clients and their families. The social work field—indeed all mental health fields—offers multiple sustaining professional choices and opportunities, and students and new graduates should keep in mind the importance of these entitlements. Those more seasoned in our profession who are looking for new experience can also seek out varied settings.

As one of our respondents put it:

I have experienced [feelings of burnout], but never tolerated them for long, hence my experience in a variety of settings. I believe this is one of the strengths of our profession/degree—I was able to move around [to varying opportunities] within the field of social work and it always felt like a brand new "career." (Respondent #7)

This social worker warded off burnout by changing professional environments, varing her focus: residential treatment with children, school-based social work, hospice, adoption home studies, and private practice. For others, of course, varied new job transitioning may feel unsettling. Again, adaptations are reflections of our individual need for creative and stabilizing expression.

All social workers, however, will want to do their best to find a work setting that values the importance of internal rotations, a safe environment, suitable time off, and opportunities for professional growth and development, and, in addition, is committed to doing *all possible* to help employees prevent burnout. Just as we teach our clients to be proactive, we also must seek work settings that are respectful of our own need to care for and protect ourselves. With this in mind, during all job interviews, it is vital to inquire about the organizational culture one is considering joining. Safety at work is nonnegotiable. Yet beyond that, providing the optimum quality of support for employees can be a difficult, if not impossible, challenge for organizations, taxing its resources of both time and money. Simply giving social workers permission to recognize the existence of burnout may be as far as some organizations can take a self-care discussion, leaving the rest up to the individual social worker. In these instances, social workers must will themselves to explore creative opportunities outside of the setting. As one respondent explained:

Our administration does acknowledge that it is very stressful dealing with adults who are very ill, medically fragile, in end-stages of life and actively dying, as well as being abused, neglected and exploited . . . but they are not really doing anything specific [no funding] to lessen the case-loads or offer other tangible means of support, other than asking frontline staff and supervisors to be more "creative" in how we support each other. (Respondent #72)

In addition to the organizations mentioned earlier, which do offer active involvement in multiple ways, creative opportunities for self-care and the support and interaction of professional colleagues can also be found in discussion groups, professional book clubs, and study groups. The latter operates similarly to a book club; members read certain articles and get together to discuss them. These discussions often lead to uplifting, meaningful, and educational professional discussions, as well as sustaining friendships. Some individuals find it valuable to participate in two or three such groups.

Your hard-won skills can also extend to other enriching organizational, educational, and creative opportunities. A skilled colleague with over 25 years of experience consults regularly with various agencies in my hometown, Philadelphia, and describes this ongoing involvement as diverse, uplifting, and meaningful. At these times, she offers direction and feedback regarding the highly complex cases presented to her. Further, she meets regularly with staff members who wish to discuss ways to enhance their professional lives.

I have also found creative "out-of-the-box" experiences to be both exciting and sustaining. A few years ago, for example, I became a clinical consultant to a local Philadelphia theatre company, meeting with directors and cast members to discuss the lives of actual clients (disguising all recognizable aspects of identity, of course) that parallel lives and events in the plays. For over 30 years I have worked with adults who have experienced emotional, physical, and sexual abuse, and my most memorable involvement in this experience was consulting work done on the highly controversial play *Blackbird*, by David Harrower (2007). *Blackbird* is a play about sexual abuse, and the deprivation, pain, isolation, estrangement, and loneliness that can lead to this horrific act. One of the most poignant moments in my professional life occurred following a *talk-back* (an opportunity for cast and attendees to talk together) for this play. As the crowd was disbursing, an audience member approached me and quietly confided that she had been sexually abused and that her assailant, a family member, refused to acknowledge this abuse. She then shared her belief that events in this play, and what she saw as "an expressed apology," would help her to heal. "Tonight, for the first time," she told me, "I see that there are those who admit that they have violated an innocent and feel genuine remorse."

More recently, I began serving on the advisory board of the award-winning documentarian Jennifer Fox, whom I have known since childhood, as she brings her first fiction feature film, *The Tale*, to life. *The Tale*, with potential to educate and inform about the pervasive nature of sexual abuse, is the true story of a young girl who was sexually abused by two of her coaches at age 13. This script, uniquely told from the conflicting points of view of Jennifer at 13 and Jennifer as an adult, sheds light on issues that those in the mental health field understand so well but the general public does not: how and why a young girl can be seduced into an abusive relationship, how and why the mind turns to denial to survive, and how prevalent this violation is.

Supervisory Support

As many of us no doubt are aware, each organization or institution is likely to have its own rules and culture. Those rules and customs can be communicated through written guidelines. However, often these rules are unwritten and are explained by a social worker's direct supervisor. Thus, the impact a supervisor has on the supervisee is profound, not only on a personal level, but also because one's supervisor in large measure represents an entire organization. Effective supervision has been proven to be an essential component in the ability to prevent and heal from burnout, with responsible supervision creating "a relationship in which the social worker feels safe in expressing fears, concerns, and inadequacies" (Bell et al., 2003 p. 468). As one of our respondents put it:

> *I meet with and am in regular contact with my supervisor. When I feel myself getting overwhelmed we meet to strategize and form a plan of attack. These meetings make me feel supported and provide some semblance of control when we acknowledge the things I/we have no control over.* (Respondent #41)

Organizations with a weekly supervision format establish a venue in which material that is ripe to create burnout is processed and normalized as part of the work of the organization. The supervisor–supervisee relationship is a complex one in which, through its time-tested delicacy, the supervisee learns there can be trust. This trust develops when each partner does the necessary preparation for time together and when the supervisor is experienced in the concentration of the social worker or those with related training and is receiving or has received high-level supervisory training. It goes without saying that mutual respect and a positive professional attitude are essential in this relationship.

Although a supervisor does not function as a social worker's therapist, per se, effective supervision and debriefing include understanding what clients touch in us, whether they are individuals, couples, families, or in other instances, boards, professional settings, and institutions. Understanding the personal impact of our different clients is greatly enhanced by a trained and compassionate supervisor who provides empathy and specific strategies and stresses the importance of self-care. An absolute commitment of confidentiality is, of course, essential. What is disclosed within the supervisory relationship can be highly personal and private, and there must be assurances that whatever is discussed will remain within a protected state of confidentiality. The finest levels of supervision enhance learning and, at the same time, ensure self-protective awareness about a balanced life. One of our respondents, herself a supervisor, had this to say:

> *My primary role is supervisor to many different clinicians, interns, and staff. When I meet with them, my focus is on them, how they maintain themselves in this field. I stress self-care, having a "life, outside of work." In whatever form that takes, this is essential to prevent burnout!* (Respondent #12)

Coworker Support

The third element of professional self-care can be found in the feeling of camaraderie derived from debriefing with a coworker. As we saw in the previous chapter, an organization can encourage coworker support through providing an enhanced break room or offsite activities, and a member of a leadership team can convene groups for supervision that multiply the benefits derived by individual attendees through strategic brainstorming. Such support derives its usefulness by allowing social workers to be with individuals who are going through similar experiences and, in this way, help and support each other. With this in mind, topical sharing by colleagues facing parallel work challenges is an essential way to implement self-care. When coworkers have experienced burnout symptoms themselves from having been "down in the trenches," they are able to recognize the signs of burnout and point these out to their colleagues, as well as offer suggestions (Oser et al., 2013).

However it occurs, it is essential for self-care that you do everything possible to develop relationships with peers and coworkers whom you trust and whose company you enjoy. Having others to collaborate with who understand your challenges and frustrations, and respond to you when you need support, balances the frustration that social work and related professions can engender. It is important to note, however, that there is a fine line between processing one's daily challenges in order to address them wisely and indulging in boundless negativity. As one of our respondents put it:

> *Negativity is something that can spread easily. I want to be positive and spread positivity. I've been in work environments where people complain and have that poor attitude about their job and clients. I do not want to be a part of that. There are frustrations in the field, but you just need to focus on the positive aspects."* (Respondent #1)

There is a reciprocal relationship between the rejuvenation found in the social self-care of enjoying time with family and friends and the replenishing that can be found in a constructive dynamic with colleagues, with different situations calling for different strategies. Several of our respondents felt that in certain clearly identifiable cases, coworker support was the most powerful means to self-care available to them. For example:

> *Yes, I enjoy time with family and friends, but peer support tends to be the most helpful. . . . This is especially true for the crisis and disaster experiences. Sharing them with family tends to transfer the trauma, so I prefer to defuse/debrief with peers. That way much of the stress is left at the scene rather than taken home with me. I've heard from many social workers over the years that, when they try vent/defuse to non-social work partners, the response they most often get is "Why don't you quit" rather than the more supportive reactions they had hoped to receive.* (Respondent #34)

As stated, channeling frustration into thoughtful political advocacy is an example of constructive self-care. For example, in the mid-1990s several Philadelphia coworkers and colleagues, from various professions representing many area institutions, each deeply frustrated by the enormity of domestic violence and the denial of this reality by religious leadership, started an interfaith, multicultural initiative, "The Sabbath of Domestic Peace Coalition" (Smullens, 2001). Our group identified clergy participation and awareness as an essential "missing link" in combating domestic violence. We met with clergy of all religious denominations in our area who welcomed us, sharing statistics, studies, and our knowledge that prayer alone cannot stop an abusive partner. We also explained why it was dangerous for a religious leader to meet with partners together when one was being abused. Since that time, the majority of the religious communities we visited have established their own groups to address this danger within their houses of worship and faith communities.

Professional Self-Care: A Case Study

Traci grew up cared for devotedly by a stay-at-home mom who had five other children. Her dad was a carpenter with strong union ties; he worked hard for his family, and although money was tight, in Traci's words, "We had all that was important. We loved each other." Traci's parents were exceptionally proud of their African American roots and taught this importance to all of their children. Whenever there were funds to spare, the family together chose art that adorned the walls of their well-cared-for home. Although they lived in an area of a large city that was rampant with gangs and drugs, Traci learned how to avoid trouble.

A quiet and reflective child, her parents called her their "star" and told her again and again that she was the model for her younger brothers and sisters, and if she "excelled and was always good, they will be too." Traci stayed to herself throughout her public school days, fearing that friendships would lead to the kind of behavior that would, in her words, "lead to danger—drinking, drugs, the kind of stuff that could hurt me and my family."

An excellent student with enormous potential, she received a full scholarship to her local Ivy League college, where once again she excelled. Here, she joined an African American sorority where, for the first time in her life, she found rewarding social contacts outside of her family. She excelled in her academics, reaching dean's list status for most of her semesters. Her scholarship, however, did not include housing; Traci lived at her home, commuting to college. Her happiest days were those when her parents allowed her, with trepidation, to spend nights at her sorority house. Traci's closest friend in her sorority entered an MSW program out of state, and because she felt so rewarded by her social work academics and training, she urged Traci to also consider the social work profession.

Traci was awarded a full scholarship to a graduate school other than the one her friend attended, and at age 20, she moved away from her hometown and her parental home. Her small stipend did not cover campus housing, but she was able to find a room and bath, with kitchen privileges, in a modest home a few blocks from her graduate school. For the first time in her life, Traci was expected to participate fully in a multicultural academic setting, and she reverted back to her youth, staying alone socially, working hard, and not participating in social activities, even when invited by the African American members of her class. She did so because she feared what she feared in her youth: getting into danger and disappointing her parents.

Traci texted both parents several times daily and spoke with them on the phone several times a week, always being warned: "The best way to stay safe is to stay to yourself." She also kept in constant touch with her siblings, who continued to see her as their adored role model and guide.

In both years of her program, Traci's field placement involved children. The first year she worked in a hospital setting with young children who had cancer; the second year, in a foster care setting. Traci was highly successful working with young children, whom she knew instinctively how to reach because of her years of care of her younger siblings. She also had enormous compassion for the young who suffered, and she stood out, academically and clinically.

Traci so excelled that the foster care agency offered her employment once she graduated, an offer she gratefully accepted. Her agency knew the importance of offering consistent training programs in house and excellent self-care opportunities. With regularity, social workers were sent to superb conferences, sometimes out of state, where all expenses were covered. Attendance was required at the in-house trainings, but when Traci was offered the opportunity to travel to conferences, she declined, always heeding her parental warning and fearing that social contacts could only lead to one thing—trouble.

She also declined the opportunity to participate in the board-sponsored monthly book club get-togethers, where dinner was provided and all present chose the novel to discuss the following month. All agency employees were invited to attend this successful, well-attended gathering, as were all board members.

During her first postgraduate year of employment, Traci was assigned work with neglectful and emotionally abusive parents to whom the agency hoped to return many of the children they oversaw. Unlike her two years in graduate school, in which Traci excelled in her work with children, this year she felt totally stymied, truly immobilized for the first time in her training as a social worker.

Traci's supervisor was skilled and caring, with over 20 years' experience as a social worker. She taught a course in the history of social work at the social work school in her community, and in addition to her teaching and supervisory responsibilities, she had client responsibilities. Through superb supervision, Traci was able to see and understand that she had been surrounded throughout her formative years by the kinds of families she was now expected to work with, families so different from her own. Keeping these families at arm's length, as if they were invisible to her, was her time-honored way of both remaining safe and continuing to live up to her parents' expectations.

Once Traci faced this, she found further relief and succor when her supervisor directed her to available avenues of peer support offered in her agency. In time, Traci branched out, developing trusting relationships with colleagues and developing friendships with people from various cultural backgrounds. A favored activity became the monthly book club. In addition, Traci gained the confidence to share her necessary progression with her parents. They, in time, were able to recognize this importance and feel pride in their oldest daughter's capabilities and self-assurance.

Questions for Reflection

- Does your organization or institution offer opportunities for self-care as an individual or those you can participate in as a group?
- Do you take advantage of these opportunities? Why or why not?

- Does your organization or institution have any official messaging about self-care in their mission statement? Would it interest you, and be advisable, to become part of a team that sees these opportunities increase?
- Does your supervisor openly discuss self-care strategies with you?
- Have you ever brought up self-care concerns with your supervisor, or do you stick to discussing case histories?
- If the quality of your self-care is not discussed with your supervisor, why do you hesitate to bring it up? Do you feel he or she does not respond because of a lack of appreciation for the urgency of preventing burnout? Do you believe that urging change within your work setting would place your supervisor or your job in peril?
- Does your supervisor, in your opinion, suffer from burnout? Does she or he engage in self-care strategies?
- Are there members of your team with whom you can discuss feelings of burnout? Do you do this as part of an officially sanctioned, regularly recurring conversation or simply as part of "water cooler" talk?
- If you are in private practice, are there fellow practitioners with whom you could see founding a self-care group?
- Are there creative "outside of the box" activities that you would like to use your professional skill to initiate with your coworkers and colleagues, within your place of employment, outside of it, or a combination?
- Are there resources outside social work and mental health professions that you would like to become involved with, using your professional skills in a different and satisfying way?
- Are there those important to you, either social workers or those not in a related field, whose professional support environ offers little or no self-care support? Would any of these questions be meaningful to them? Would talking together about mutual concerns be beneficial?

Chapter 6

Self-Care in the Personal, Social, and Physical Arenas

In this chapter, we will discuss the remaining three arenas of self-care: the personal, including psychological, emotional, mental, and spiritual dimensions; the social, including partners, family, and friends; and the physical. I want to point out, once again, that none of the self-care strategies that will be presented are done so prescriptively. You will not find one iota of "must" in the following pages, other, of course, than you must care for YourSelf. You also know, if you read the Acknowledgments & Reflections pages earlier, that what I described in early pages of this book is representative of what I will now discuss. My sharing had a twofold purpose: There was much I wanted to acknowledge and express gratitude for, but, as important, I wanted to encourage you to experience springboards for your own personal self-care strategies—your necessary, individual, selective gifts to YourSelf.

At this point in your reading, you well know what research makes abundantly clear: effective self-care strategies are very individual—what works for one person may not work for another. However, when we integrate gifts to our Selves that are wise for us, experiences of joy and grace can take us to another plane, one that can both protect us from fatigue and eradicate it. With this steadying influence comes an opportunity to look inward, face difficult personal truths about ourselves and others, and through this process learn and grow.

Personal self-care strategy selections provide all of us in mental health and related professions with a greater ability to see, hear, and feel what our clients (as well as our friends and loved ones!) are trying to tell us about their own journeys and lives and their hopes and dreams. As important, they renew energy to continue to work toward greater societal opportunities for the most vulnerable among us.

Because these choices are exceedingly personal, this chapter includes more excerpts from our respondents than some of the other chapters. In this way, you will experience firsthand not only what works for others, but also how it looks and feels when self-care strategies are ones that you may find to be protective, stabilizing, and uplifting.

Personal Self-Care

Psychotherapy, Counseling, Consultation

As we saw during our earlier discussion of burnout, existing research documents that the childhoods of mental health professionals contain a relatively high prevalence of trauma and family dysfunction in terms of more conflict and less cohesion (Elliott & Guy, 1993). Researchers have postulated that such family dynamics, which lead to an internalization of the caretaking role, are a first step toward entry into the mental health field (Guy, 1987).

This, of course, is not the case in the lives of all social workers. However, if you did face less than optimal experiences in your family of origin that are thought to be particularly influential in the choice of a helping profession such as social work (Fussell & Bonney, 1990), the effects can actually be quite subtle. For example, if you are feeling the impact of the lack of validation in your formative years, you may be less able both to use the self-care strategies presented in this book and to prioritize your life schedules and relationships around receiving that self-care. Further, in all likelihood you began your graduate work without realizing the link between your childhood and your desire to help others, or even to understand that what you experienced in your home was unsettling and painful.

Social workers and other mental health professionals, whose education involves an appreciation of "an examined life," usually become open and more aware. As you move forward in your academic training and your contact with clients, be they individuals you see in session or other settings, your social work education most likely will lead to introspection and further self-awareness, where you become more and more comfortable asking yourself questions such as, "What are my clients touching in me about my own life—past and present?" "Are there avenues about either my past and present life, or both, that should be explored in more depth?"

This openness and awareness may well contribute to data stating that our home environments during formative years have been more dysfunctional than those of people who choose other professions; for there are difficult, painful, even terrifying, days or periods in all lives; and all people make wrong choices, have regrets and lost dreams, and may be surrounded by, as well as make, tragic mistakes.

Unlike the majority of professions, however, ours and related ones place emphasis on the importance of facing the truths about our lives to increase our effectiveness. This emphasis does much to alleviate the kind of exhaustion that leads to burnout. According to Norcross (2000), a high percentage of mental health practitioners who do go into therapy, benefit from their therapy, and, as a result, find their work and life exceedingly fulfilling. In his words:

> It is well established and widely known that the majority of mental health professionals . . . have sought personal therapy. What is equally well established but not widely known is that (a) more than half of [mental health practitioners] following completion of their training utilize the very service they provide and (b) the vast majority . . . 90% plus—rate the outcomes of personal therapy quite positively. (p. 712)

One of my classmates, whom I'll call Julie, was born with a congenital heart defect when pediatric medicine was relatively primitive. Julie lived the first eight years of her life in and out of hospitals, a time when doctors wrongly believed that young children had immature nerve endings and therefore felt no pain. In addition, parental visitation was restricted to limited hours. The hospitalized children did their best to support and find comfort in each other. As Julie grew older, although she found even the thought of physical pain intolerable, she decided to devote herself professionally to children who had been traumatized as she had. To ensure her own continued growth and to counteract vicarious trauma, compassion fatigue, and countertransference, Julie entered psychotherapy. She not only had a gifted career, but also achieved her goal of making a real difference in children's lives.

Julie's experience underscores earlier research by Fussell and Bonney (1990) noted that the painful childhoods of mental health practitioners "enhanced, not extinguished, continuing interest in people." This study presented the likelihood "that resolution of childhood pain requires a protracted struggle—one that continues well into adulthood." It warns against "inappropriate nurturance and the patient's acceptance of the sick role," urging clinicians "to use their own basic therapeutic strategies." It also stressed the positives of "interest in people," emphasizing the relationship between "childhood ambiguity" and " curiosity," and concluding that "curiosity is essential to an accurate conceptualization of psychopathology" (p. 511).

Even those who have not been aware of personal difficulties within their own families are surely aware of the suffering of many in their communities, their cities, their general society, and beyond. Examining closely how these realities influenced you and your view of life's possibilities can also serve you well as you work to develop your professional perspective and strengths.

In other words, to grow toward excellence in your chosen field, the hard work of knowing yourself as fully as possible can actually prefigure your own personal and professional success. As such, professional counseling, consultation, and psychotherapy are important vehicles to consider as personal self-care strategies. However, they are not the only ones. They can be used in concert with religious or spiritual practices on one hand or an active process of self-reflection, such a journaling, on the other. What all of these personal self-care strategies have in common is the transmutation of personal pain (which many students entering the field are unaware they carry) into empathic skills. In this way, with the proper practices and mind-set in place, rather than seeing one's dysfunctional childhood as a deficit, or even a curse, it can be seen as an opportunity to learn to become more insightful and compassionate and help one blossom into a fuller professional.

Many recognized schools of thought have produced effective approaches to helping our clients. Today, for myriad reasons, many clinicians have moved from a psychodynamic approach, in which underlying unconscious and interpersonal forces that impede growth are examined and recognized, to therapies that are behavioral or cognitive, or a combination of the two, in order to alter self-defeating behaviors and attitudes. Regardless of theoretical orientation or emphasis, when a practitioner in the mental health field takes a history and hears of a client's life, he or she cannot help but be involved and touched; introspection and self-awareness remain vital safeguards against burnout.

The self-care strategies one teaches a client are the same ones that serve a professional well. To quote Dr. Nancy Braveman, who provides trauma-focused treatment to sexually abused children:

> More and more I find myself using the same coping skills . . . I teach children and caregivers in therapy sessions. Namely diaphragmatic breathing and progressive muscle relaxation to help with the physiological components of stress. In addition, I practice "cognitive coping" strategies, e.g., becoming more aware and tolerant of my thoughts, feelings and actions in the present moment. (N. Braveman, personal communication, November 14, 2014)

Dr. Braveman continues with a strategy discussed previously that I teach my clients (and use myself), which I call "InnerSelf Dialogue" (Smullens, 2002). To quote Dr. Braveman,

> If/when I notice myself having an "unhelpful" or inaccurate thought, I offer myself a replacement thought. This can decrease my stress level and help me better deal with challenging clinical (or personal) situations. I try not to resist, avoid or deny the uncomfortable feeling, but to acknowledge, tolerate

and move through it. When I can accomplish this, I am empowered to make better decisions using my head, instead of being ruled or directed by my feeling of anxiety, fear, anger, etc. (N. Braveman, personal communication, November 14, 2014)

Religious and Spiritual Dimensions

When we turn to the religious and spiritual dimensions of self-care, we move to an area that draws immediate and passionate responses—whether yea or nay—from many social workers and health care professionals. Nonetheless, religious self-care strategies, such as prayer and worshipful communion, and spiritual self-care strategies, such as meditation and mindfulness, merit attention in a social worker's panoply of options, in large part because many social workers do use prayer or other rituals to alleviate their burnout and report success from such efforts. Our discussion here will be brief and always ecumenical, or to put it another way: "In God's house there are many mansions," and if you are uncomfortable and don't want to be in a mansion, that's absolutely fine, too.

To say that a self-care activity is religious or spiritual in nature may make it seem more complicated or involved than it actually is. In the words of one respondent: "I pray every day in the mornings and evenings and I usually ask for wisdom, understanding, and peace for myself and everyone I meet during the day. This has also been helping me consistently for a while" (Respondent #50).

Such a practice may offer the practitioner the support she or he needs to be present in the workplace. As Dombo and Gray (2013) pointed out, a helpful spiritual practice can counter burnout in a unique way:

> *Burnout can interfere with the ability to sense inner goodness in clients, especially difficult clients. It is hard to listen without judgment when there has been trauma. When the worker is experiencing vicarious trauma, it is difficult if not impossible to be fully present for the client.* (p. 94)

Personal self-care strategies of this type can range from the most traditional religious practices, such as religious reading, attending religious services, and keeping the Sabbath, to nontraditional practices, such as meditation and making gratitude lists. I cannot stress enough that finding meaning beyond oneself can occur in a many different ways and in creative combinations. As one of our respondents explained:

> *Prayer is very important to me and this actually goes along with exercise. Many times my alone/exercise time is when I choose to engage with God and that makes it even more restful and filling. I pray daily and the positive effects are ongoing.* (Respondent #7)

One of the personal self-care strategies of the religious or spiritual type that came up most frequently among our respondents was the practice of mindfulness. Upon entering the mainstream of Western culture, mindfulness has undergone a translation that can sometimes be confusing. Originally derived from Buddhist practice, *mindfulness* is an "intentional, accepting and non-judgmental focus of one's attention on the emotions, thoughts and sensations occurring in the present moment" (Zgierska et al. 2009, p. 267). In this sense, mindfulness can be seen as an umbrella term for developing, as Jon Kabat Zinn described it: "new kinds of control and wisdom in our lives, based on our inner capacities for relaxation, paying attention, awareness and insight" (quoted in McGarrigle & Walsh, 2011, p. 214). Thus, mindfulness is an increased awareness of the present moment while creating a calm and contented state (Cox & Steiner, 2013). How is this practice of mindfulness understood by today's social worker and health care practitioners, and how does it benefit us?

One social worker interviewed mentioned changing his private practice to a mindfulness-based psychotherapy method and going to professional trainings to achieve this focus (Respondent #78). One mentioned having a mindfulness application on her smartphone that helped her establish some clarity before she began the frantic bustle of her day (Respondent #32). The effects of mindfulness training have had a positive impact on several of our respondents:

> *I am a mindfulness trained therapist so I try to engage in regular practices at work and home. It definitely helps with the burnout and it is refreshing and motivating to continue with what I do. I am not sure how long the effects of it last because I practice mindfulness daily.* (Respondent #20)

✳ ✳ ✳

> *I practice mindfulness and meditation along with yoga. I believe faith is a spiritual feeling. Practicing these techniques and living in the moment help to counteract the feelings of burnout.* (Respondent #70)

Dombo and Gray (2013) suggested that the common descriptor of all such strategies is "anything that helps the social worker to find meaning beyond self, meaning in relationships, and meaning in clinical practice" (p. 95). I have observed an increased interest in labyrinths to promote mindfulness and alleviate anxieties in the past several years. Unlike a maze, a labyrinth has no confusing, unsettling obstacles to overcome. One merely concentrates on remaining on the patterned path, which has a clear beginning and end.

Recently, my client, an MSW student who consulted me due to persistent anxieties, described her first experience labyrinth walking before her exams as "uplifting, even spiritual":

> *I walked twice. The first time I also meditated and felt calmer. The second time I just walked. My anxieties seemed to melt; I felt better about my abilities to deal with the pressures in my life; and I was able to concentrate on the lovely day. This was a far better choice than drugs, which in numbing my anxieties also numb me.*

One common denominator of those who engage in either traditional religious or spiritual practices is that these approaches to self-care combat feelings of powerlessness and promote centeredness. They encourage focus on those things that bring relief from the constancy of problems to be addressed and help one both put difficulties, complications, and obstacles in perspective and rise above them to restore and replenish strength and energy. In this way, they assist all health care professionals at any given moment to be able to act instead of react and to listen for inspiration that comes from what some conceptualize as a deeper or higher self and thus avoid being weighed down by fear and confusion. As examples: One who feels pressure when cooking can make one simple dish, ask others to bring dishes, and focus on the pleasure of loving friends and family being together. One who feels drained and saddened by caring for clients who will soon die can concentrate on the comfort he or she brings them. One who is ill, with little chance for recovery, can realize that he, himself, is fine, even as his body fails him.

The practice of gratitude, of counting of one's blessings despite fear, loss, pain, and disappointment, can be regarded as an aspect of mindfulness but merits concentration in its own right in our discussion of self-care. As you know, the Acknowledgment section of this book is my personal expression of gratitude to those who have added so much depth, caring, direction, and hope to my life,

Gratitude extends to *all* that life brings that has enriched and inspired: health and restored health; shared love and friendship, comfort, and joy, even when there is loss; a shared meal with those close to us—as well as an exquisite sunrise and sunset, a tenderly cared for garden, fallen snow glistening in the sunlight—beauty that too often we do not take time to either notice or appreciate.

The importance and challenges of those closest to us in relationship to our self-care will be discussed in the conclusion of this chapter; however, in our concentration on mindfulness and gratitude as important self-care opportunities, the significance of touch cannot be overlooked. This includes sexual activity, either alone or with a partner. With fulfilling sexual expression, the world seems a better place, where one feels able to cope with problems large and small far more easily.

Again and again, my clients who live alone have confided that what they miss most is a loving touch from one who cares. All caring physical contact—a friend who takes your hand, puts an arm around you, or shares a hug in a reciprocal manner—promotes a fulfilling and stabilizing sense of well-being, Of course, through the ages, pets have been a consistent source of comfort, warmth, and caring—providing companionship, one to care for, and a sense of well-being.

Journaling

For many social workers, mindfulness and gratitude come together in the self-care practice of journaling. As a gift for one of my daughters who had recently had a baby, I asked family friends to write down some of their best advice for good parenting. One friend responded, "Write down the sweet little things your little one does and says because, if you do not, you'll forget." In this context, we can recast this advice as: Remember to keep and protect your own experience. When there is something in our profession that really moves you that you see, or some little success that truly brightens your day, you can write about it, from your heart, your head, your gut. Remember, your writing does not have to be grammatically correct. Just let it flow. Through this process you may find, as one of our respondents did, that your recorded experiences will come together in a very helpful and meaningful way:

> I always encourage the writing of any unusual incident reports and/or use of journaling as another way to get things out, process things, and leave them behind. Much of my professional writing has been done . . . to externalize the stress and to impart practical lessons learned to others who may follow me in doing similar work. Much of my consulting, my presentations at professional conferences, and clinical supervision I provide others also allows similar reflection and release for me. (Respondent #34)

We often do not know how we feel about something until we begin to write about it, and the process of writing helps us both to clarify and to understand. However, if after writing about something, we remain confused and baffled, this is a sign that your inner guide, which Otto Rank refers to as a force within the Self, is telling you that it would be wise to talk to someone, possibly a supervisor or professor. Or perhaps you will want to turn to a resource outside of your academic or work setting, such as a trusted friend or professional. Respecting your inner guide is strategically essential to self-care.

You can also write about people and experiences other than your clients, your sessions, and your experiences on the job; you can write about all things that mean something to you: a news story, a film, music, whatever touches something within that speaks to you (or, put differently, motivates your "inner voice") and makes you feel it would be wise and productive to record your thoughts and reactions.

You can also, of course, journal about your self-care activities. Students in a recent section of the class, "Foundation Social Work Practice" at the University of Louisville were given an assignment to keep "a biweekly self-care journal in which they chronicled the actions they took to keep their emotional, physical, psychological, social, and spiritual selves healthy during the semester" (Moore et al., 2011, p. 547). In their journals, they discussed the activities they undertook and why, what the specific issues these activities were meant to address, and how these activities contributed to their well-being. The consistent results of this journaling were a reduction in stress and an improved ability to focus on schoolwork and clients, in addition to momentum to further implement additional self-care strategies (Moore et al., 2011).

Social Self-Care: My Self and My Family

Respondents indicated time and time again that one's intimate circle, especially partners and family members, often received the brunt of a social worker's irritability, depression, and lethargy resulting from burnout. But just as these close and crucial relationships may be negatively affected, they can also be wellsprings of life-giving waters with mutually fulfilling results. One respondent reported:

> I also enjoy time with my adult children, who are also very supportive emotionally—having experienced the effects of my career firsthand. They all try very hard to help me NOT be a "social worker" on my time off! Being outdoors, in the woods, campgrounds or state parks, away from crowds or large groups of people, is a big stress reliever for me. (Respondent #72)

It is a break to be with your own children and not ask, "How do you feel about this?" It is a break to tell yourself, "If they want to tell me they will, and I can just enjoy our walk, our cooking, reading, our time. They are not my clients. They are my children." It is always fun to hear them say, if we slip, "Hey, Mom (or Dad), stop 'social working' me."

All of us who work in a field of mental health know exceedingly little free personal time, and it is essential that we give ourselves permission to relax. Or, in Rankian terms, that *we will our Selves* to find time for what we personally need to restore, such as a night out with friends, window shopping, visiting thrift shops for innovative "finds," signing up for music or dance lessons, or planning a trip to a spa. It is important to know that we do not always have to improve our intellectual capacity by doing "meaningful things," such as seeing documentaries or engaging in heavy reading. If we enjoy it, we can read a pulpy magazine, or spend an entire day watching any kind of films we enjoy and then, perhaps, a thriller late into the night. In other words, we can have fun!

I think you will enjoy this example of self-care: A good friend, a nurse who works in a highly charged and demanding academic center, browses in thrift shops as one way to relax. During these excursions, she regularly finds gifts for herself and her mother, who lives hundreds of miles away. After sending her mom a large purse she knew she would enjoy, she received an admonishing call: "You shouldn't have been so generous!" her mother told her sternly. "Mom, what are you talking about? It's only a purse." After a few seconds of silence, her mother asked, "Did you look inside the zippered part of the purse?" "No," my friend responded, "Was something there?" "Yes, there was," was the response—"five hundred dollars in cash, and a pair of aquamarine and gold earrings." (As a follow-up, my friend called the shop to try to trace ownership of what was found. She was told that the purse was part of a huge "clean-out" of several homes, that the thrift shop should have been more diligent, and that "finders are keepers.")

The following is one of my own indulgent, fun, self-care strategies: Every several weeks, I buy a very large oatmeal raisin cookie at my favorite bakery, put it into my briefcase, computer bag, or whatever I am carrying, and take myself to a favorite movie theatre on a late afternoon when few are in attendance. There I buy a large cup of coffee or tea (depending on my mood), find a quiet corner of the theatre, and forget about everything else but these two wonderful hours; time just for me. I love intricate dramas and mysteries, but sometimes I pick a comedy, for as we all know, laughter is a marvelous way to take an uplifting holiday from life's stressors and demands.

The most essential factor is creating enjoyable and productive self-care strategies that work for both you and your family (although most likely they will not involve finding cash and aquamarine earrings!), strategies you will want to return to with enough regularity to reap their benefits. In this creation, omit "I have to!" Someone may say, "My husband (or wife) and I both enjoy a juicy drama. Sometimes we relate what we see to my work, and he/she better understand the demands I face." For some couples, this choice would fall into a definitive "Give Me A Break!" category. As one respondent explains, "My husband and I stick to comedies for movies, so we can laugh. No drama; everyday life is drama! Again, the effects last because I continuously engage in them" (Respondent #3).

As seen in the previous examples, burnout can be alleviated by approaching it head-on or by acknowledging the burnout implicitly and engaging in other activities. Below is another successful adaptation:

> My husband and I are fortunate enough to have a day during the week that we commit to each other. We began doing this several years ago and it has made an incredible difference in our lives and our connection to each other. We might do errands, hike, walk, or just stay at home. Individual and marriage counseling . . . did help, not because we dealt with my burnout necessarily, but because it re-focused me on that primary relationship with my partner. (Respondent #7)

Just as there are times when a couple's closeness, compatibility, and companionship help prevent and alleviate exhaustion and fatigue, there are also times, very sad ones, especially if children are involved, when to save one's strength and emotional well-being, one must leave a marriage. In the words of a former client, a social worker, who leads a large and vibrant department in industry:

> For years I did everything I possibly could to persuade my husband that joint counseling was essential—but to no avail. Every accomplishment made him angry and jealous, and he would lash out and demean me brutally. I was beginning to burn out at work. I could not concentrate, or plan, or lead. I was the main breadwinner, and our twins in junior high were suffering from the constant anger and anxiety in our home. Finally, with a thorough examination of myself [and], my family needs—our lives and futures—I realized that my children and I both needed and deserved a different quality of life and that an end of . . . my marriage was the only rational choice.

Social Self-Care: Friends

Self-care as it relates to the next largest circle of acquaintances outside of our immediate family can walk a very interesting fine line between the self-care we receive by sharing and debriefing with our peers (discussed in the last chapter) and the social self-care derived by engaging in activities with friends who know nothing about social work and mental health practices—or with those in our field where all discussions about work challenges are off limits. We know, of course, that our social interaction does not come from professional relationships with clients. What we may not be aware of is the degree to which social workers (as well as those in all professions!) who make their work their entire lives may be contributing to their own burnout. The constant, persistent processing of cases and problems at work and continuous discussions about work after office hours are draining and depleting. In the words of one of our respondents:

> *I am trying to make friends outside of work so we can have other things to talk about. Talking with a friend from work about stuff at work works a little bit but just watching a movie helps a lot. Shopping with a friend helps a lot too. These positive feelings can last usually until the next shift. It's similar to the feelings after working out.* (Respondent #24)

In today's world, we now have the opportunity to easily experience the presence of friends in our lives who live at great distances. Reaching out to others through social media, for example, can reverse the effects of loneliness and burnout. At a point in life when there isn't a friend nearby who will understand what you're saying or what you're going through, or, for your own personal reasons, you feel more comfortable communicating honestly with those who do not live near by, this kind of connection can be especially positive and reassuring. As an example, one respondent reported the same self-care effects of connection and lightness of heart when communicating with friends digitally: "I communicate with friends daily—albeit it [is] often via Facebook or email, since so many [friends] now are spread out across the country. The effects are long lasting" (Respondent #2). Once again, the important thing to ascertain is whether the effects of this specific or any other self-care activity are positive for you. If so, then it is an effective strategy.

Dr. Geoffrey Greif, professor of social work at the University of Maryland, talks about categories of friendships that contribute to a life experience. By the time one reaches adulthood, most no longer require a "best friend," one who helped us feel whole and validated during adolescence (Greif, 2008). Instead, Greif defines the types of friends we do need into the following four categories: "must," "trust," "just," and "rust," friends. A "must" friend is the most intimate, one whom we call with essential news. "Trust" friends are a larger group: There is caring, but the intimacy, perhaps because time does not allow it, is not as deep. "Just" friends are those whose company one just enjoys, while "rust" friends have a long, shared history—remembering things about each other's past chapters—and may drift in and out of each other's lives.

I would suggest a fifth category: "dust friends," those one lets go of by design or default. An important social self-care strategy involves a decision to let go of a friendship. In fact, one of the most important social self-care strategies is knowing when it is necessary to remove depleting and toxic "friendships" from your environment.

In a particularly interesting exchange, the following question was asked on the questionnaire: "What self-care strategies have you tried that have not worked for you in terms of promoting resilience or improvement of mood/ outlook?" One respondent replied,

> Hanging out with people who are in a miserable space. Misery loves company, but I don't love staying miserable, so I have reduced a lot of friendships and stick to people who don't just withdraw from my energy but can offer a reciprocal positivity! (Respondent #3)

When reading this comment, however, please note the point also made earlier: Offering feedback and support, being there as a friend confronts and works through a challenge or difficulty, is an act of caring—the polar opposite of relentless complaints and self-pity, persistent put-downs, condescension, and insulting behavior.

Physical Self-Care

As Akande, van Wyck, and Osagie (2000) pointed out, the human body was designed for physical activity. Students and professionals in the mental health field often sit for long periods of time; our work and study demand it. A regular exercise program and proper nutrition are crucial to preventing burnout that can result from a lack of physical activity. Many respondents discussed the value of exercise—"it's a sanemaker" (Respondent #6), one of them said—as well as the difficulty we may have committing to a regular exercise program.

Two respondents described their weekly routines as follows: "I do the exercise and good eating all week all the time (minus weekend sinful food and wine time). The effects last because I continuously engage in them. When these methods stop working, it is time for vacation" (Respondent #3).

> Physical activity has been critical to my ability to do this work. There was a time when I got up at 4 A.M. to walk because my days were so full of work and children. Even on a day-to-day basis the impact . . . [has been] HUGE—the days I exercised my energy was exponentially more, and I think everyone in my life was served more positively. I still exercise and it's still critical, but I don't have to do it at 4 A.M. anymore. The effects last as long as I stay committed to the exercise, so I don't go without it. (Respondent #7)

Another critical aspect of physical self-care that was reported was the need for getting enough sleep. As we noted in the previous chapter regarding the need to take vacations and sick days to avoid professional burnout, gone are the days when those we report to should value exhaustion, due to lack of sleep, as a positive characteristic of an employee. Again, in the words of one respondent:

> *I am generally ready to take on the day if I go to sleep early enough and wake up refreshed. Then I feel awake, alert, energetic, and happier. Conversely, if I do not get enough sleep I may experience headaches, depression, and tightness of my neck and shoulder muscles. That is when I know I do not feel ready to take on the day's challenges.* (Respondent # 59)

Physical self-care is not limited to the specifics of diet, exercise, and sleep. It is essential to have regular medical and dental checkups necessary to help ensure good health and address any necessary additional care, illness we may be unaware of, or the possibility of a potential illness. Often, to supplement our physical well-being, the services of other professionals, such as a masseuse or chiropractor, may be helpful. The deciding factor for maintaining an auxiliary physical self-care practice is the same as any other essential aspect of self-care—if it works for you, it is right for you. To borrow Lee and Miller's (2013) definition, effective self-care creates "[r]evitalization and generation of energy: sustaining energy, encouragement, and hopefulness through and about one's work [which] is central to maintaining both effectiveness and a sense of professional well-being" (p. 101).

Personal, Social, and Physical Self-Care: A Case Study

Maddy and Stephanie became friends during each of their first marriages, supported each other during their divorces, and were both delighted and amazed to learn that they had remarried men who had once been childhood friends but had lost touch with each other once they completed high school.

The four formed an instantaneous bond. Theirs was a relationship of regular dinners and shared activities; the constancy seemed important to all four. There was also much interest in and devotion to each other's children. There were signs of differences in the couples' parenting and communication styles, but in the interest of the friendship, this was never discussed. Specifically, Maddie seemed to need to keep her two sons exceptionally close to her, resenting when their friendships, in her words, "intruded on family time." Unlike Stephanie, who discussed all things relating to their two daughters with her husband, asking for his input as they addressed family challenges together, Maddy's husband gave her complete control of family matters.

An extremely unsettling and unexpected disruption in the friendship came several years after the friendship began. Even as a young girl, Stephanie's daughter Joyce had always had a huge crush on Maddy's son, Jason. One evening, when both were in their senior year of high school, Jason made it clear to Joyce that he was interested in knowing her differently than as "a kid who my parents know." The four teenage friends, now all in high school, spent a terrific evening together; and Joyce, knowing that there had been a dramatic shift in how Jason acted toward her, was elated and looked forward to his promised text the next day.

Instead, in the early morning after this get-together, Stephanie received a stunning telephone call from Maddy: "I am going to get to the point quickly," she told her. "I have known for a long time that Joyce is attracted to Jason, but I want to warn you that Joyce's heart will be broken by him." Stephanie asked Maddy if Jason were ill or if there were a problem she was unaware of. "Of course not," Maddy responded coldly. "Jason is no way near the point of having a close relationship with a girl. He needs first and foremost to remain close to us until he knows what he wants out of life. This is just not the time for him to date someone like your daughter, who is looking for a serious boyfriend."

Stephanie was shocked at the implications, intrusiveness, and rudeness of this call but tempered this feeling by asking calmly: "Isn't this a matter between Joyce and Jason?"

"No, it certainly is not," responded Maddy, who before hanging up the phone said tersely: "I never before told you this, Stephanie, but I see you as a far too liberal and lenient parent."

A few hours later, Maddy's husband Mark telephoned, telling Stephanie that he wanted Sid and her to know that he and Maddy were canceling all future dates. Later that day, Joyce received a text from Jason, telling her that he did not deserve a person "as pretty and terrific as you." Joyce was initially very shaken, and because she trusted both of her parents, she decided to discuss the entire experience with them. Theirs was a long conversation, and tears were shed by Joyce. But the time together led to Joyce's expressed understanding: "Jason has a lot of growing up to do, and his Mom is not going to make that easy."

Stephanie did not rebound as quickly as her daughter. She could not shake her upset about the abrupt nature and unkindness of both telephone calls from supposedly loyal friends. Her sadness became so intense that she began to withdraw from her family. Predictably, her work as a high school guidance counselor began to suffer. Although Stephanie had confidence in her parenting, she began to ruminate about Maddy's criticism of her. And she also found herself incensed and enraged about the implications of her supposed friend's words about her daughter. Not surprisingly, Stephanie found it hard to focus on the students who relied on her and began to truly believe she had nothing to offer them. Knowing that something was very wrong, the compassionate principal of Stephanie's school urged her to see her doctor, but Stephanie, unable to accept this suggestion, pushed herself to work daily, as she became less and less able to concentrate. Finally, after two months of Stephanie's ignoring her husband's plea that she see her doctor, he insisted that his wife schedule a medical consultation. Stephanie finally acquiesced. Following a complete physical exam and the necessary accompanying blood tests, her doctor referred her to a clinical social worker with experience working with professionals suffering from burnout.

During this work, Stephanie was able to mourn the loss of one she considered a good and trustworthy friend and realized how necessary it was for her to let go of this relationship. Just as important, Stephanie began a weekly exercise program, combined with yoga, which she had been meaning to do for years. She also began to have monthly massages and added journaling to her self-care program. She realized that Maddy and Mark needed to be placed in the "dust" friend category. With the passage of time, both Stephanie's professional life and her life at home rebounded, and slowly, once again, she began to thrive.

Questions for Reflection

- Have you engaged in personal psychotherapy, counseling, or consultation of a related nature? Do you feel that the effects were beneficial? If so, in what ways?
- Were your efforts to receive therapy related to a crisis in your life? Did you initiate them in a proactive manner?
- If you are receiving counseling or therapy currently, do you discuss the symptoms of burnout with your therapist frequently, occasionally, or not at all?
- Have you ever turned to a supervisor, mentor, professor, or friend to discuss the genesis of your burnout and ways to alleviate it? Has this been helpful? If so how? If not, why not?
- Do you engage in any religious or spiritual practices of self-care? Is there one or more that help you feel more resilient and optimistic?
- Do you keep a journal currently? Can you see yourself keeping a self-care journal, even for a limited time, to track your progress and note successful self-care activities?

- Are there members of your family or social circle who seem especially adept at relieving your symptoms of burnout? Do you have relationships with another adult with whom you find it draining to share time?
- How do you feel your physical condition contributes to burnout, if at all? Have you ever sought a successful physical self-care strategy? If you have found one or more, how would you describe them?
- Do you engage in regular sexual activity, either alone or with a partner?
- Do you express your affection and caring with good friends through touch?
- Do you have or have you ever considered a pet as a source of comfort and a sense of well-being?
- Do you believe that any of these reflections may be meaningful to those important to you, either in social work and related professions, or not? Would discussion about shared concerns and direction be beneficial?

Conclusion

Boundaries and Self-Care

"People will disappoint you. Life will hurt you. But if you have something that is completely yours to invest in, something you are passionate about, you can rise above pain and find personal joy and loving connection. For me that something is social work." (From my journal, the summer of 1977)

While researching this book, I found the above reflection and in this, the concluding chapter, I would like to follow it with the wise, incisive, and articulate words of one of our respondents:

> I remember agreeing to do the best I can. I did not agree to being under-paid, or treated as "less than" because I'm a social worker. I did not agree to change the world, my clients, or any other institution. I agreed to advocate and serve as best I could. (Respondent #44)

As we reflect on the three attendant syndromes of burnout we have studied in this book, compassion fatigue, countertransference, and vicarious trauma, as well as the four arenas of self-care that provide their antidote in the professional, personal, social, and physical realms, we can understand the self-awareness, self-discipline—in essence, the hard work—that leads to and perpetuates healthy boundaries and attitudes about our clients, our work, and ourselves. This is more readily achieved if we muster the courage to understand and see how some problems faced by clients lead to the necessity to more carefully evaluate and understand ourselves and our own choices.

Most who enter our profession have a compelling, even burning, desire to work tirelessly toward a fairer, more just society for all, especially those who have suffered deeply, have been marginalized, and have received the fewest advantages. You well know, however, that as a social worker the work toward this goal is never ending; and there will often be forces working in dead opposition to what we know are the best opportunities for our clients on their journeys toward hope, healing, opportunity, and success.

Therefore, part of self-care is learning to accept that, as we work toward change and success with our clients, there will be things we cannot change in the setting that employs us, as well as in our clients' choices. We must accept that some clients, despite opportunities, are not ready for growth and that some will not change. We must accept that positive individual forward motion, despite obstacles, is up to the client.

In honoring the separation—the necessary boundary—between ourselves and our clients, we develop patience and the determination to respect another's process. For even with motivation, change is hard for everyone, and change is a slow and tedious process. We also must remember that what can seem a failure is actually a success. The client who went for an interview, but was not accepted for the job, has tried. The courage to try is something wonderful to build on, and we would be wise to also remember this framing in our own lives.

As our skills sharpen, we realize the importance of perspective, calm, and common sense to greater extents. To quote an astute social work respondent:

> My feelings [include] yes, being upset with lack of resources, support for the families and youth that I engage with, certainly a lack of funding at both the Federal and State level, which has been ongoing as long as I have been in this field. I am an optimist however, and at the end of the day, I attempt to treat one family at a time, one youth at a time, and do my best during each session, [each] interaction! In this field, especially within child welfare, a person must remain strong, a belief that all will get better but at the same time, much is not within our control, so once you accept this fact, then the work comes naturally . . . My other adage is if you are working harder than your youth, family, then something is terribly wrong, so [by keeping that in mind] I have been able to maintain this way of working and why I have survived this long. (Respondent #49)

The frustrations faced by social workers and all mental health professionals underscore the importance of valuing and caring for ourselves in the ways that are right for each of us. Commitment to integrating self-care in our lives protects the passion and dedication that led us to our profession. Without this union, there cannot be efficacy. Without it, we cannot hold on to the understanding, to the truth, that we have not failed if our clients do not succeed. We have not failed if our work settings and our communities do not offer necessary resources to those who need them the most. With our determined integration of self-care and dedication, despite disappointments, we will continue to advocate for what is just and necessary, taking defeats seriously but never personally.

The years have taught me that if we cannot integrate these important attitudes and boundaries in both our personal and professional lives and, in this way, protect our strength, energy, and self-respect, we will be unable to say "yes" to a healthy and fulfilling life. Without this determination—what I think of as a promise to ourselves—there will be marvelous opportunities before our very eyes that remain invisible in every facet of our lives. Said in a different way: We will sabotage our opportunities for success.

To care well for ourselves, we must say "yes" to using our sick days and vacation time, decide how many hours of work per week are too many, and leave an abusive work setting. If we find no fulfillment in our present professional setting, we must do all we can to find a new setting. Perhaps a different sector within our field will be a wise choice, or perhaps we want to express our professional knowledge and passion in other avenues.

The ability to say "yes" to health and opportunity cannot happen if we cannot say "no." To maintain our self-respect and safeguard our health, the wisdom of the words that began the concluding chapter. "I did not agree . . . to be treated 'less than,'" must be an integral part of our professional attitudes and actions. This understanding will make it possible to help our clients to see that always saying "yes" will not ensure being loved, accepted, treated well, or never abandoned, for without the self-respect that comes with choice and balance, without knowing one has the right to say "no," one will never find mutual respect.

Appropriate self-care involves knowing that our profession is not our life, and our clients can never compensate for any pain or deprivation we or those we love and care about may have known. Our clients replace no one; they compensate for no one. They are not and never can be part of the personal world we must work hard to carve out for ourselves. As important, the insights and boundary understanding central in self-care underscore that we fail our clients (as well as overwhelm them) if our determination for their growth is greater than their own.

The reasons that many in social work and related professions easily give so much naturally are individual to each, as well as complex; but they often involve pain in our own lives, pain we have watched a love one, a family, a community, a society endure, and often our own pain as well.

Watching suffering, knowing suffering firsthand usually leads to one of two adaptations: One becomes cold, callous, uncaring, and even cruel, or one develops a deep understanding and compassion toward others and innately knows how to express this in a helpful and healing way. In other words, one becomes what I have come to think of and describe as a "natural social worker."

Natural social workers exist in every profession, including homemakers and professional volunteers. I have seen again and again the good they often do, working hard and honorably. They are those who work hard and honorably. They are neither power hungry nor conniving. They can both lead and follow and, when they lead, they do not dominate or control. They are those who, when crises comes, muster the strength to build again and help others to do the same.

During the nine-year period I served on the Board of Overseers at my graduate school alma mater, the Overseers initiated the Crystal Stair Award, a title based on the Langston Hughes poem "Mother to Son," which was written in 1922 (Hughes, 1994). The award honored and recognized "natural social workers," those of any profession or volunteer capacity, who work tirelessly toward individual opportunity and a more just and equitable society. When one who is compassionate, a true healer, turns toward social work education and training, he or she then builds on an innate and passionate resolve and chooses a road toward deep professional fulfillment, despite obstacles and impediments. Even with ever-present deterrents, there is a promise implicit in a social work degree—to continue, to the best of our abilities, to advocate for resources for those whose voices are not heard—those whose suffering is unseen or ignored—those regarded by large segments of the population as invisible, unworthy, unimportant.

An essential component of this commitment is the understanding that the personal, professional, and political are one, a continuum, each woven into the other. Just as our individual self-care assertion protects us from depletion, our social work promise—based on inextricable links between the personal, professional, and political—underscores the foundation and protects the future of our profession. This integration constitutes an essential component of self-care, combating burnout. Passivity, when life can be so cruel for others and options for opportunity remain limited, can be energy depleting. Thoughtfully planned, professionally directed assertion leads to renewed energy.

With the importance of this ever in mind, as part of our commitment to our clients, as well as for own self-care, we can continuously work assertively to educate, to raise awareness that our clients deserve far more opportunities for success and autonomy. Despite the negativity that may surround us, we can, in Rankian terms, *will our Selves* never to feel defeated and never to stop advocating: To accomplish this, we can adopt some of the examples described in past pages or use these examples to stimulate our own direction. We can speak out by writing letters to the editor, by going online, and saying and writing what we believe. We never know who will be influenced by our conversations or what we write—wherever we write, wherever we speak. Common sense and optimism raise consciousness; and sound ideas, stated articulately and with conviction, are contagious. One never knows who, in the world of government or philanthropy, will be touched deeply and moved toward action and activism by thoughtful and compassionate stands we take on behalf of our clients and our profession.

An active membership in the National Association of Social Workers, nationally and in your home state, can help you identify these opportunities. Community involvement and political activities are vital creative opportunities that go hand in hand with professional commitment. Further, these efforts renew energy and alleviate the feelings of helplessness and powerlessness that can lead to burnout.

I do not think it will surprise you that, through the years, I have often thought of the client who wrote me the note that opened this book. Yes, she spoke and, yes, she healed. Hers was not, and had never been, an easy road. For social workers and our clients, for all of the reasons noted, those you know so well, it never is and never will be. Yet, despite everything, our proud and historic profession asks us for an enduring promise of commitment. Being there, in our fullest and healthiest capacity, is the gift of Self that makes it possible for this promise to be kept.

References

Agllias, K. (2012). Keeping safe: Teaching undergraduate social work students about interpersonal violence. *Journal of Social Work Practice: Psychotherapeutic Approaches in Health, Welfare and the Community, 26*(2), 259–274.

Akande, A., van Wyck, C., & Osagie, J. E. (2000). Importance of exercise and nutrition in the prevention of illness and the enhancement of health. *Education, 120,* 758–772.

Alkema, K., Linton, J. M., & Davies, R. (2008). A study of the relationship between self-care, compassion satisfaction, compassion fatigue, and burnout among hospice professionals. *Journal of Social Work in End-of-Life & Palliative Care, 4*(2), 101–119.

American Psychiatric Association. (2013). *Diagnostic and statistical manual of mental disorders: DSM-5* (5th ed.). Arlington, VA: American Psychiatric Publishing.

Ashford, J., LeCroy, C. W., & Lortie, K. L. (2006). *Human behavior in the social environment: A multidimensional perspective* (3rd ed.). Belmont, CA: Thompson.

Bell, H., Kulkarni, S., & Dalton, L. (2003). Organizational prevention of vicarious trauma. *Families in Society, 84,* 463–470.

Bourassa, D. B. (2009). Compassion fatigue and the adult protective services social worker. *Journal of Gerontological Social Work, 52,* 215–229.

Burke, R. J., & Cooper, C. L. (2008). *The long work hours culture: Causes, consequences and choices.* Bingley, United Kingdom: Emerald Group Publishing.

Burns, K. (2011). 'Career preference', 'transients' and 'converts': A study of social workers' retention in child protection and welfare. *British Journal of Social Work, 41,* 520–538.

Chrestman, K. R. (1995). Secondary exposure to trauma and self-reported distress among therapists. In B. H. Stamm (Ed.), *Secondary traumatic stress: Self-care issues for clinicians, researchers, and educators* (pp. 29–36). Lutherville, MD: Sidran.

Coleridge, S. T. (1965). *The rime of the ancient mariner. The annotated ancient mariner.* New York: Clarkson N. Potter.

Corcoran, K. J. (1987). The association of burnout and social work practitioners' impressions of their clients. *Journal of Social Service Research, 10*(1), 57–66.

Cox, K., & Steiner, S. (2013). *Self-care in social work: A guide for practitioners, supervisors, and administrators.* Washington, DC: NASW Press.

Dane, B. (2002). Duty to inform: Preparing social work students to understand vicarious traumatization. *Journal of Teaching in Social Work, 22*(3/4), 3–20.

Dombo, E. A., & Gray, C. (2013). Engaging spirituality in addressing vicarious trauma in clinical social workers: A self-care model. *Social Work & Christianity, 40*(1), 89–104.

Elliott, D. M., & Guy, J. D. (1993). Mental health professionals versus non-mental-health professionals: Childhood trauma and adult functioning. *Professional Psychology: Research and Practice, 24*, 83–90.

Figley, C. R. (1995). *Compassion fatigue: Coping with secondary traumatic stress disorder in those who treat the traumatized.* Levittown, PA: Brunner/Mazel.

Fox, R. (2003). Traumaphobia: Confronting personal and professional anxiety. *Psychoanalytic Social Work, 10*(1), 43–54.

Freud, S. (1958). The dynamics of transference. In J. Strachey (Ed. & Trans.), *The standard edition of the complete psychological works of Sigmund Freud* (Vol. 12, pp. 97–108). London: Hogarth Press. (Original work published 1912)

Freudenberger, H. J. (1974). Staff burn-out. *Journal of Social Issues, 50*(1), 159–165.

Freudenberger, H. J. (1975). The staff burn-out syndrome in alternative institutions. *Psychotherapy, 12*, 73–82.

Fussell, F. W., & Bonney, W. C. (1990). A comparative study of childhood experiences of psychotherapists and physicists: Implications for clinical practice. *Psychotherapy, 27*, 505–512.

Gerdes, K. E. (2011). Empathy, sympathy, and pity: 21st-Century definitions and implications for practice and research. *Journal of Social Service Research, 37*, 230–241.

Gibson, F., McGrath, A., & Reid, N. (1989). Occupational stress in social work. *British Journal of Social Work, 19*, 1–6.

Greif, G. (2008). *Buddy system: Understanding male friendships.* Oxford, UK: Oxford University Press.

Guy, J. D. (1987). *The personal life of the psychotherapist.* New York: John Wiley & Sons.

Hamama, L. (2012). Burnout in social workers treating children as related to demographic characteristics, work environment, and social support. *Social Work Research, 36*, 113–125.

Harrower, D. (2007). *Blackbird.* New York: Dramatists Play Service.

Hughes, L. (1994). *The collected poems of Langston Hughes.* New York: Vintage Books.

Humphrey, K. R. (2013). Using a student-led support group to reduce stress and burnout among BSW students. *Social Work with Groups, 36*, 73–84.

Kernberg, O. F. (1965). Notes on countertransference. *Journal of the American Psychoanalytic Association, 13*, 38–56.

Kim, H., Ji, J., & Kao, D. (2011). Burnout and physical health among social workers: A three-year longitudinal study. *Social Work, 56*, 258–268.

Kramer, R. (1995). The birth of client-centered therapy: Carl Roger, Otto Rank, and "the beyond." *Journal of Humanistic Psychology, 35*(4), 54–110.

Lee, J. J., & Miller, S. E. (2013). A self-care framework for social workers. *Families in Society, 94*, 96–103.

Lieberman, E. J. (1985). *Acts of will: The life and work of Otto Rank*. New York: Free Press.

Lloyd, C., King, R., & Chenoweth, L. (2002). Social work, stress and burnout: A review. *Journal of Mental Health, 11*(3), 255–265.

Martin, U., & Schinke, S. (1998). Organizational and individual factors influencing job satisfaction and burnout of mental health workers. *Social Work in Health Care, 28*, 51–62.

Maslach, C. (1993). Burnout: A multidimensional perspective. In W. B. Schaufeli, C. Maslach, & T. Marck (Eds.), *Professional burnout: Recent developments in theory and research* (pp. 19–32). Washington, DC: Taylor & Francis.

Maslach, C., Jackson, S., & Leiter, M. (1996). *Maslach burnout inventory manual*. Palo Alto, CA: Consulting Psychologists Press.

McGarrigle, T., & Walsh, C. A. (2011). Mindfulness, self-care, and wellness in social work: Effects of contemplative training. *Journal of Religion & Spirituality in Social Work, 30*, 212–233.

Moore, S. E., Bledsoe, L. K., Perry, A. R., & Robinson, M. A. (2011). Social work students and self-care: A model assignment for teaching. *Journal of Social Work Education, 47*, 545–553.

Newell, J. M., & MacNeil, G. (2010). Professional burnout, secondary traumatic stress, and compassion fatigue: A review of theoretical terms, risk factors, and preventive methods for clinicians. *Best Practices in Mental Health: An International Journal, 6*(2), 57–68.

Norcross, J. C. (2000). Psychotherapist self-care: Practitioner-tested, research-informed strategies. *Professional Psychology: Research and Practice, 31*, 710–713.

Oser, C. B., Biebel, E. P., Pullen, E. P., & Harp, K. L. (2013). Cause, consequences, and prevention of burnout among substance abuse treatment counselors: A rural versus urban comparison. *Journal of Psychoactive Drugs, 45*, 17–27.

Pearlman, L. A., & Mac Ian, P. S. (1995). Vicarious traumatization: An empirical study of the effects of trauma work on trauma therapists. *Professional Psychology: Research and Practice, 26*, 558–565.

Pearlman, L. A., & Saakvitne, K. W. (1995). *Trauma and the therapist: Countertransference and vicarious traumatization in psychotherapy and incest survivors*. New York: W. W. Norton.

Polster, E., & Polster, M. (1974). *Gestalt therapy integrated: Contours of theory and practice*. New York: Vintage Press.

Radey, M., & Figley, C. R. (2007). The social psychology of compassion. *Clinical Social Work Journal, 35*, 207–214.

Regehr, C., & Cadell, S. (1999). Secondary trauma in sexual assault crisis work: Implications for therapists and therapy. *Canadian Social Work, 1*, 56–70.

Rogers, C. (1974). Client-centered and symbolic perspectives on social change: A schematic model. In D. A. Wexler & L. N. Rice (Eds.), *Innovations in client-centered therapy* (pp. 465–496). New York: John Wiley & Sons.

Scarf, M. (1995). Unfinished business: Pressure points in the lives of women. New York: Ballantine.

Schwartz, R. H., Tiamiyu, M. F., & Dwyer, D. J. (2007). Social worker hope and perceived burnout. *Administration in Social Work, 31*(4), 103–119.

Siebert, D. C., & Siebert, C. F. (2007). Help seeking among helping professionals: A role identity perspective. *American Journal of Orthopsychiatry, 77*(1), 49–55.

Skovholt, T. M., Grier, T. L., & Hanson, M. R. (2001). Career counseling for longevity: Self-care and burnout prevention strategies for counselor resilience. *Journal of Career Development, 27*, 167–176.

Smullens, S. (2001). Counseling the clergy on how to help victims of domestic violence. *Annals of the American Psychotherapy Association, 4*(6), 15–18.

Smullens, S. (2002). *Setting yourself free: Breaking the cycle of emotional abuse in family, friendships, work and love.* Far Hills, NJ: New Horizons Press.

Smullens, S. (2003, Fall). Developing an emotional sense of direction: A therapeutic model for the treatment of emotional abuse. *Annals of the American Psychotherapy Association, 6*(3), 17–21.

Smullens, S. (2010). The codification and treatment of emotional abuse in structured group therapy. *International Journal of Group Psychotherapy, 60*, 111–130.

Stamm, B. H. (1995). *Secondary traumatic stress: Self-care issues for clinicians, researchers, and educators.* Lutherville, MD: Sidran.

Taylor, P. G., & Cheung, M. (2010). Integration of personal/professional self (IPPS) through reflective/experiential learning. *Journal of Teaching in Social Work, 30*, 159–174.

Tosone, C., Minami, T., Bettman, J. E., & Jasperson, R. A. (2010). New York City social workers after 9/11: Their attachment, resiliency, and compassion fatigue. *International Journal of Emergency Mental Health, 12*(2), 103–116.

Tosone, C., Nuttman-Shwartz, O., & Stephens, T. (2012). Shared trauma: When the professional is personal. *Clinical Social Work Journal, 40*(2), 231–239.

Turner, F. J. (Ed.). (1986). *Social work treatment: Interlocking theoretical approaches* (3rd ed.). New York: Free Press.

Winnicott, D. W. (1949). Hate in the counter-transference. *International Journal of Psychoanalysis, 30*, 69–74.

Zgierska, A., Rabago, D., Chawla, N., Kushner, K., Koehler, R., & Marlatt, A. (2009). Mindfulness meditation for substance use disorders: A systematic review. *Substance Abuse, 30*, 266–294.

Index

W

Walsh, C. A., 62, 65, 66, 86
War veterans, 18–19
Well-being
    defined, 62
    self-care and, 17
Will, as inner force, 58

Winnicott, D. W., 14
Workshops, 70
Writing. *See* Journaling

Z

Zgierska, A., 86